The Jewish Messiah

D0913810

The Jewish Messiah

Dan Cohn-Sherbok

T&T CLARK
EDINBURGH

T&T CLARK LTD
59 GEORGE STREET
EDINBURGH EH2 2LQ
SCOTLAND

Copyright © T&T Clark Ltd, 1997

All rights reserved. No part of this publication may be reproduced,
stored in a retrieval system, or transmitted, in any form or by any means,
electronic, mechanical, photocopying, recording or otherwise,
without the prior permission of T&T Clark Ltd.

First published 1997

ISBN 0 567 08586 4

British Library Cataloguing-in-Publication Data
A catalogue record for this book is available from the British Library

BM
615
.C560
1997

Typeset by Fakenham Photosetting Ltd, Fakenham, Norfolk
Printed and bound in Great Britain by The Cromwell Press, Melksham

JESUIT - KRAUSS - McCORMICK - LIBRARY
1100 EAST 55th STREET
CHICAGO, ILLINOIS 60615

To Lavinia

Contents

Acknowledgments

I would like to acknowledge my indebtedness to a number of important books from which I obtained information as well as source material: Robert M. Seltzer, *Jewish People, Jewish Thought: The Jewish Experience in History*, London, 1980; John Drane, *Introducing the New Testament*, Tring, 1986; Abba Hillel Silver, *A History of Messianic Speculation in Israel*, Gloucester, Mass., 1978; Shlomo Avineri, *The Making of Modern Zionism: The Intellectual Origins of the Jewish State*, New York, 1981; Arthur Hertzberg, *The Zionist Idea: A Historical Analysis and Reader*, New York, 1969; Joseph Klausner, *The Messianic Idea in History*, London, 1956; *Encyclopedia Judaica*, Jerusalem, 1972.

Biblical quotations are from the Revised Standard Version of the Bible, copyright © 1946, 1952, 1971 by the Division of Christian Education of the Churches of Christ in the USA. Used by permission. Quotations from the Apocrypha and the Pseudepigrapha are from R. H. Charles, *The Apocrypha and Pseudepigrapha in English*, London, 1913.

Chronological Table

Patriarchal period	c. 1900–1600 BCE
Exodus from Egypt	c. 1250–1230 BCE
Period of the Judges	c. 1200–1000 BCE
Period of the United Monarchy	c. 1030–930 BCE
David	1010–970 BCE
Division of the Kingdoms	c. 930 BCE
Amos	fl. 8th Century BCE
Hosea	fl. 8th Century BCE
Destruction of the Northern Kingdom	722 BCE
Isaiah	fl. 8th Century BCE
Micah	fl. 8th Century BCE
Zephaniah	fl. 7th Century BCE
Jeremiah	fl. 7th–6th Century BCE
Destruction of the Southern Kingdom	586 BCE
Babylonian exile	586–538 BCE
Ezekiel	fl. 6th Century BCE
Return of the Exiles	538 BCE
Rebuilding of the Temple in Jerusalem	c. 520–515 BCE
Second Temple Period	c. 515 BCE–70 CE
Second Isaiah	fl. 6th Century BCE
Haggai	fl. 6th Century BCE
Zerubbabel	fl. 6th Century BCE
Zechariah	fl. 6th Century BCE
Malachi	fl. 5th Century BCE
Daniel	c. 2nd Century BCE

Jesus	fl. 1st Century BCE
New Testament written	c. 50–90 CE
Jewish rebellion against Rome	66–70 CE
Mishnaic (Tannaitic) period	c. 100 BCE–200 CE
Simeon bar Kochba	fl. 2nd Century
Mishnah compiled	c. 200
Talmudic (Amoraic) period	c. 200–600
Jerusalem Talmud compiled	c. 5th Century
Moses of Crete	fl. 5th Century
Babylonian Talmud compiled	c. 6th Century
Medieval period	c. 600–1600
Karaism founded	c. 760
Abu Isa al-Ispahani	fl. 8th Century
Serene	fl. 8th Century
Yudghan of Hamadan	fl. 8th Century
Eldad Ha-Dani	fl. 9th Century
Saadiah Gaon	882–942
Hasdai Ibn Shaprut	915–970
Benjamin of Tudela	fl. 12th Century
First Crusade	1096
Second Crusade	1145–1147
Solomon ibn Gabirol	1021–1056
Rashi	1040–1105
Judah Halevi	1078–1141
Third Crusade	1189–1190
Abraham bar Hiyya	fl. 12th Century
Moses Maimonides	1135–1204
David Alroy	fl. 12th Century
Bahya ben Asher	fl. 13th Century
Establishment of the Inquisition	c. 1230
Abraham Abulafia	1240–1291
Solomon ben Abraham Adret	1235–1310
Levi ben Gerson	1288–1344
Moses Botarel	fl. 14th–15th Century
Hasdai Crescas	1340–1412
Disputation of Tortosa	1413–1415
Simeon ben Duran	1361–1444
Isaac Abrabanel	1437–1508

Expulsion of the Jews from Spain	1492
Solomon Molko	1500–1532
Asher Lämmlein	c. 1500
David Reuveni	fl. 16th Century
Mordecai ben Judah Dato	1525–1591
Isaac Luria	1534–1572
David ben Solomon ibn Abi Zimra	fl. 16th Century
David Gans	1541–1613
Hayyim Vital	1542–1620
Manasseh ben Israel	1604–1657
Shabbetai Tzevi	1626–1676
Nathan of Gaza	1643–1680
Abraham Cardozo	c. 1630–1706
Baruchiah Russo	fl. 18th Century
Jonathan Eybeschuetz	1690–1764
Jacob Emden	1697–1776
Modern period	c. 1700–present
Moses Hayyim Luzzatto	1707–1747
Jacob Frank	1726–1791
Baal Shem Tov	1700–1760
Yehuda hai Alkalai	1798–1878
Zwi Hirsch Kalischer	1795–1874
Moses Hess	1812–1875
Leon Pinsker	1821–1891
Reform movement founded	c. 1850
Theodor Herzl	1860–1904
Abraham Isaac Kook	1865–1935
Conservative movement founded	c. 1895
Menahem Mendel Schneerson	1902–1994
Modern orthodoxy founded	c. 1905
Reconstructionist movement founded	c. 1935
The Holocaust	1942–1945
Founding of the State of Israel	1948
Humanistic movement founded	c. 1965

Introduction

For thousands of years the Jewish people has longed for messianic deliverance; sustained by this belief the community has endured persecution and suffering, confident that they will ultimately be rescued from earthly travail. Yet with the rise of science and the growth of secularism, this fervent conviction has lost its force for many modern Jews. No longer does it seem conceivable that a divinely appointed redeemer will arise to deliver the Jewish nation and bring about the transformation of history.

Nonetheless, for some members of the community the belief in the coming of the Messiah continues to retain its hold on Jewish consciousness. A dramatic illustration of the enduring character of this conviction has recently been manifest within one of the major sects of Hasidism. Over the last few years a significant number of Lubavicher Hasidim have proclaimed that their spiritual leader (*Rebbe*) – Menahem Mendel Schneerson – is the long-awaited Messiah even though he did actually die in 1994.

During his lifetime the *Rebbe* had established a world-wide empire of disciples, spread Torah Judaism to places where it had never been known, energized Jewish education, and led numerous irreligious Jews to observance of Jewish law. On this basis, a growing body of messianic Hasidim became convinced that the period of messianic deliverance was imminent. As a result a massive wave of leaflets and booklets was produced, announcing the *Rebbe* as the Messiah.

When the *Rebbe* suffered a stroke, his followers were not deterred; indeed, the *Rebbe*'s incapacity fuelled the flames

of messianic enthusiasm. His illness was invested with
redemptive significance: the suffering servant in Isaiah 53
was perceived as being a reference to the *Rebbe*'s debili-
tated state. According to a number of his disciples, the
Rebbe would not die, despite his stroke; and they prayed
for his recovery daily, reciting: 'May our master, teacher
and Rabbi the King Messiah live for ever!'

Even the *Rebbe*'s death did not daunt those who were
convinced of his Messiahship. He would return! In the
view of one Israeli newspaper, those who had lost faith in
the *Rebbe* were like the worshippers of the golden calf who
had given up hope of Moses' return from Mount Sinai.
Within a few months of the funeral, two volumes
appeared, explaining the grounds for continuing faith in
his Messiahship.

Eventually, as time passed, a number of messianists
became convinced that the *Rebbe* had not in fact died: in
their view he remains alive but concealed. Hence what
happened on 3 *Tammuz* 5754 (the Jewish date of his
death) was an illusion. The *Rebbe*'s corpse, they argued,
was a test for carnal eyes; but in truth there was no passing
away or leave-taking at all. Some followers of the *Rebbe*
have even gone so far as to use incarnational terminology
in describing his mission. During his lifetime, the *Rebbe*
was referred to as the 'Essence of the Infinite'; today
some Lubavicher Hasidim talk of him as 'Master of the
Universe'.

Here then is the most recent manifestation of the
continuation of the heart-felt longing of the Jewish
nation: Menahem Mendel Schneerson is the last link in a
long chain of messianic pretenders stretching back over
twenty centuries of Jewish history. The aim of this volume
is to provide an overview of the Jewish quest for messianic
deliverance from biblical times to the present day, and to
assess whether such a religious belief is now superfluous.
Chapter 1 thus commences with an account of the history
of the promise of a future redemption in Scripture.
Beginning with God's revelation to the patriarchs, the
chapter outlines the message of the eighth-century prophets

who foretold the destruction of the Jewish people while reassuring the nation that there would be a future ingathering of the exiles. The theme of divine deliverance continued in the ministries of later prophets who foresaw a time of divine deliverance of the nation; in their view, the Israelites would not be cut off forever.

The account of the nation's longing for restoration continues in Chapter 2 with a presentation of the messianic idea as found in the Apocrypha and Pseudepigrapha. In the Apocrypha there are frequent references to the ingathering of the exiles and a future world. Dating from after the destruction of Jerusalem, the Pseudepigrapha are filled with messianic descriptions. After the country was devastated, the Jews were bereft of a homeland – in their despair the nation longed for a messianic deliverer of the house of David who would lead them back to Zion. Basing their beliefs on prophecies in Scripture, the Jewish people foresaw a period of redemption in which earthly life would be transformed and all nations would bow down to the one true God. In these works the chain of messianic deliverance is described in detail.

As Chapter 3 demonstrates, such a utopian vision animated rabbinic reflection about God's providential plan for his chosen people. According to rabbinic speculation, this process would involve the coming of a messianic figure (Messiah ben Joseph) who would serve as the forerunner of a second Messiah. This second Messiah would bring back all the exiles to Zion and complete earthly existence. Eventually at the end of the messianic era, all human beings would be judged: the righteous would enter into heaven whereas the wicked would be condemned to eternal punishment. This eschatological vision served as a means of overcoming the nation's despair over the loss of its sacred homeland.

Chapter 4 continues this presentation of the history of the nation during the Second Temple period by focusing on Jesus' messianic claims. It appears that a Jewish sect of Christians emerged during the years of unrest following Herod's death in 4 BCE. In consonance with messianic expectations of this period, these believers expected Jesus as the Messiah to bring about the fulfilment of human history. According to the New Testament, Jesus spent most of his life in Galilee where he acted as a healer, exorcist and itinerant preacher who proclaimed the imminent arrival of the Kingdom of God. After he was put to death during the reign of Pontius Pilate, his followers believed he had risen from the dead, appeared to them, and promised to return to usher in the period of messianic rule. The Jewish population, however, refused to accept Jesus as the Messiah; in their view he failed to fulfil the messianic role as portrayed in Scripture and post-biblical sources.

As Chapter 5 illustrates, messianic longing intensified in the years following the destruction of the Temple, and in 132 CE the military leader Simeon bar Kochba was viewed by many Jews as the long-awaited Messiah. However, when his rebellion against Rome was crushed, Jews put forward the year of redemption. In the middle of the fifth century another messianic figure, Moses from Crete, stated that he would lead Jewish inhabitants of the island back to the Holy Land. After his plan failed, Jews continued to long for a future return and their aspirations are recorded in various midrashic collections. Subsequently Jewish scholars attempted to ascertain the date of the final redemption on the basis of biblical texts. In addition, during this period various pseudo-Messiahs appeared and the traveller, Eldad Ha-Dani, brought news of the Ten Lost Tribes. Later such messianic expectation increased as Jews faced persecution and death during the time of the Crusades.

As Chapter 6 explains, during the next two centuries various Jewish writers attempted to predict the date of final redemption on the basis of the Book of Daniel. In addition, during these years a number of false Messiahs appeared on the Jewish scene, and as time passed other calculators continued to speculate about the coming of the Messiah. Prominent among the mystical works of this period was the *Zohar*, which contains numerous calculations about the coming of the messianic age. Finally, in the thirteenth century, another messianic figure, Abraham Abulafia, attracted a wide following from Jews who longed for a return to Zion. Thus medieval Jews, like their ancestors, yearned for a release from the bondage of exile and looked to the advent of the Messiah as a means of deliverance.

The early modern period witnessed this same aspiration for redemption. As Chapter 6 demonstrates, during the fourteenth and fifteenth centuries various messianic tracts were written, and in the next century the tradition of messianic calculation was continued by various Jewish sages. During this century a number of pseudo-Messiahs appeared who also claimed to bring about a new era. Undaunted by their failure, messianic calculators of the seventeenth century persisted in their computations. Prominent among the messianic speculators of this century was Manasseh ben Israel, who believed that the hour of deliverance was near.

The Cossack Rebellion which began in 1648 and devastated Polish Jewry heightened the belief that the coming of the messianic age was near at hand. As Chapter 8 explains, in this milieu the arrival of the self-proclaimed messianic king, Shabbetai Tzevi, was announced by his disciple Nathan of Gaza. Throughout the world, Jews were persuaded that the Messiah had come and flocked to his court. Yet, when Shabbetai converted to Islam rather than face death, his apostasy evoked dismay among his followers. Nonetheless, a number of his disciples, including Nathan of Gaza, continued to believe in his messiahship. Subsequently a schismatic group of his disciples (the *Doenmeh*) broke away from mainstream Judaism, and later the Shabbatean movement was led by Jacob Frank whose followers subscribed to a heretical version of the Shabbatean tradition.

With the conversion of Shabbetai Tzevi, the Jewish preoccupation with messianic deliverance ceased to preoccupy the nation. Nonetheless, as Chapter 9 illustrates, a number of religious Zionists – including Yehuda hai

Alkalai, Zwi Hirsch Kalischer and Abraham Isaac Kook –
maintained that it was necessary to rebuild the Holy Land
in anticipation of the advent of the Messiah. Opposed to
such a reinterpretation of Jewish messianism, Orthodox
critics argued that the quest to create a Jewish settlement
in Palestine is a usurpation of God's will. Distancing
themselves from such religious preoccupations, secular
Zionists such as Moses Hess, Leon Pinsker and Theodor
Herzl maintained that the creation of a Jewish homeland
is the only solution to the problem of anti-Semitism.
Unconvinced by this argument, liberal Jews maintained
that Jewish prejudice could be overcome if the Jewish
population assimilated into the countries in which they
lived.

In modern society, however, most Jews have found it
increasingly difficult to accept the traditional scheme of
messianic redemption. Supernatural ideas about the
advent of the Messiah and the unfolding of a divine
providential plan have seemed increasingly implausible in
the light of scientific knowledge and the growth of secularism. As a consequence, a fundamental revision to
Jewish theology is now necessary; as outlined in the final
chapter, such a new theology of Judaism envisages religious doctrines as ultimately human in origin. Given the
inevitable subjectivity of religious belief, contemporary
Jews should free themselves from the religious absolutism
of the past. Rather than posit the coming of a messianic
figure who will bring about the reign of justice and
peace on earth, they ought to direct their energies to
creating a better world without appealing to supernatural
intervention.

1

The Biblical Messiah

In the Hebrew Bible, God declared to Abraham, Isaac and Jacob that their descendants would inherit a land of their own. In later biblical history, Scripture foretells of a future redemption which will be brought about through an anointed agent of the Lord. Such a kingly figure, the early prophets maintained, would be a descendant of David – his throne would be secure for all time. Eventually there arose the view that the house of David would rule over both the Northern and Southern Kingdoms as well as neighbouring peoples. Later the eighth-century prophets such as Amos and Hosea predicted the destruction of the nation because of its iniquity, yet in accordance with the divine promise they prophesied that there would be an ingathering of the exiles and the dominance of the Israelites over surrounding nations. Such suffering was to serve as a means of moral reform: Israel is to endure devastation before such redemption can take place. Then the Lord will have compassion upon his chosen people and return them to their former glory. This message of destruction and restoration continued in the ministries of later pre-exilic prophets: for such figures as Isaiah, Micah, Zephaniah and Jeremiah God would in time deliver the Israelites – they would not be cut off forever. A new redemption, they proclaimed, would bring about a new spiritual life. In the post-exilic period, the message of hope and consolation was a predominant theme: again the prophets reassured the nation that God would be reunited with his people and Zion would undergo future glory. The theme of a future redemption was echoed in

the Psalms: there, too, the promise of a future king
became a predominant theme. Finally, the Book of Daniel
predicts the coming of a divinely appointed deliverer –
the Son of Man is to be given dominion over all the
earth.

From the Patriarchs to Pre-exilic Prophecy

The term 'Messiah' is an adaptation of the Hebrew *Ha-
Mashiah* ('the Anointed'); in time it came to refer to the
redeemer at the End of Days. Although there are no
explicit references to such a figure in the Torah, the
notion of the redemption of the Jewish nation is alluded
to in the promises made to the patriarchs. Thus, in the
Book of Genesis, Abraham is told that he will be the father
of a multitude:

> And I will make of you a great nation, and I will bless you, and
> make your name great, so that you will be a blessing. I will
> bless those who bless you, and him who curses you I will curse;
> and by you all the families of the earth shall bless themselves.
> (Genesis 12:2–3)

Again, in Genesis 26:3–4 Abraham's son Isaac is told that
his descendants will be as numerous as the stars and that
through them all nations will be blessed:

> I will give all these lands, and I will fulfil the oath which I
> swore to Abraham your father. I will multiply your descen-
> dants as the stars of heaven, and will give to your descendants
> all these lands; and by your descendants all the nations of the
> earth shall bless themselves.

Finally, Isaac's son Jacob is reassured in a dream that his
offspring will be as the dust of the earth, the source of
God's blessing to all peoples:

> And he (Jacob) dreamed that there was a ladder set up on
> the earth, and the top of it reached to heaven; and behold,
> the angels of God were ascending and descending on it! And
> behold, the Lord stood above it and said, 'I am the Lord, the
> God of Abraham your father and the God of Isaac; the land
> on which you lie I will give to you and to your descendants;

and your descendants shall be like the dust of the earth, and you shall spread abroad to the west and to the east and to the north and to the south; and by you and your descendants shall all the families of the earth bless themselves.'
(Genesis 28:12–14)

Although these verses do not express a clear conception of the Messiah, they form the background to the evolution of the doctrine of the deliverance of the nation.

In the Book of Samuel the notion of redemption through a divinely appointed agent was explicitly expressed: here Scripture asserts that the Lord had chosen David and his descendants to reign over Israel to the end of time. Thus 2 Samuel 23 proclaims:

Now these are the last words of David:
The oracle of David, the son of Jesse,
... the anointed of the God of Jacob ...
The God of Israel has spoken,
the Rock of Israel has said to me:
When one rules justly over men,
ruling in the fear of God ...
Yea, does not my house stand so with God?
For he has made with me an everlasting covenant,
ordered in all things and secure. (2 Samuel 23:1, 3, 5)

In this passage David is depicted as the anointed in the sense that he was consecrated for a divine purpose.

Of similar significance are the verses in 2 Samuel and 1 Chronicles where Nathan the prophet assured the king that his throne would be established for all time and that his throne would be secure forever. Speaking to David about the construction of the Temple, he declared:

Thus says the Lord of hosts, I took you from the pasture, from following the sheep, that you should be prince over my people Israel; and I have been with you wherever you went, and have cut off all your enemies from before you; and I will make for you a great name, like the name of the great ones of the earth. And I will appoint a place for my people Israel, and will plant them, that they may dwell in their own place ...
(2 Samuel 7:8–10)

This early biblical doctrine assumed that David's position

would endure through his lifetime and would be inherited by a series of successors who would carry out God's providential plan. With the fall of the Davidic empire after the death of King Solomon, there arose the view that the house of David would eventually rule over the two divided kingdoms as well as neighbouring peoples. In the words of the eighth-century prophet Amos:

'In that day I will raise up
the booth of David that is fallen
and repair its breaches,
and raise up its ruins,
and rebuild it as in the days of old;
that they possess the remnant of Edom
and all the nations who are called by my name,'
says the Lord who does this. (Amos 9:11–12)

Yet despite such a hopeful vision of Israel's future, the pre-exilic prophets were convinced that the nation would be punished for its iniquity. Warning the people of impending disaster, Amos spoke of the Day of the Lord when God would unleash his fury against those who had rebelled against him. This would not be a time of deliverance, but of destruction: 'Woe to you who desire the day of the Lord!', he declared. 'Why would you have the day of the Lord? It is darkness, and not light' (Amos 5:18). Here the prophet portrayed such a day in the most negative terms:

Therefore thus says the Lord, the God of hosts, the Lord:
'In all the squares there shall be wailing;
and in all the streets they shall say, "Alas! alas!"
They shall call the farmers to mourning
and to wailing those who are skilled in lamentation,
and in all vineyards there shall be wailing;
for I will pass through the midst of you'. (Amos 5:16–17)

For Amos the Day of the Lord will be bitter – feasts will be turned into mourning and songs to lamentation (Amos 8:10). Those who are secure in Samaria will go into captivity, and Israel will be driven into exile (Amos 6:7; 7:17).

For Amos, then, the Day of the Lord is the necessary result of sin: this fearful prediction serves as the backdrop to deliverance. Before Israel can be redeemed, the nation is to suffer exile, destruction and slaughter. Only after such terrible events will the house of David be restored to its former glory and the kings of the house of David rule over the ten tribes. At the time of salvation there will be an ingathering of the exiles and Israel will rule over all foreign powers.

Like Amos, Hosea believed that God would punish his people for their sinfulness. Predicting the end of the Northern Kingdom, he prophesied that the people will be exiled to Assyria and Egypt:

> They shall not remain in the land of the Lord;
> but Ephraim shall return to Egypt,
> and they shall eat unclean food in Assyria. (Hosea 9:3)

Such suffering, however, is to serve as the means to moral reform. Israel is to endure the pangs of childbirth before redemption can come (Hosea 13:13). Such chastisement is to bring about repentance and dedication to the covenant. Then the Lord will have mercy on his chosen people and exalt them among the nations:

> Come, let us return to the Lord;
> for he has torn, that he may heal us;
> he has stricken, and he will bind us up.
> After two days he will revive us;
> and on the third day he will raise us up,
> that we may live before him.
> Let us know, let us press on to know the Lord;
> his going forth is sure as the dawn;
> he will come to us as the showers,
> as the spring rains that water the earth. (Hosea 6:1–3)

There is thus a direct link between destruction and redemption. According to Hosea, although the people shall be deprived of their king this situation will change once the Israelites mend their ways and return to the Lord:

> For the children of Israel shall dwell many days without king
> or prince, without sacrifice or pillar, without ephod or

teraphim. Afterward the children of Israel shall return and seek the Lord their God, and David their king; and they shall come in fear to the Lord and to his goodness in the latter days. (Hosea 3:4–5)

Echoing Amos, Hosea predicted that the Day of the Lord will be great and abundant: it will result in earthly prosperity and bliss:

I will be as the dew to Israel;
he shall blossom as the lily,
he shall strike root as the poplar;
his shoots shall spread out;
his beauty shall be like the olive,
and his fragrance like Lebanon.
They shall return and dwell beneath my shadow,
they shall flourish as a garden. (Hosea 14:5–7)

The captives and the exiles shall return to their own land, and in another passage Hosea prophesied that the order of nature will be fundamentally altered: 'And I will make for you a covenant on that day with the beasts of the field, the birds of the air, and the creeping things of the ground; and I will abolish the bow, the sword, and war from the land; and I will make you lie down in safety, (Hosea 2:18). Here in embryonic form is the concept of perfect peace in the end of days. Drawing faith from the closing chapters in the history of Northern Israel, both Amos and Hosea predicted a future age in which the glories of the Lord would be manifest in the land.

From Isaiah to the Fall of the Southern Kingdom

The Book of Isaiah begins by explaining that what follows is an account of the prophesies of Isaiah concerning Judah and Jerusalem. In the first prophetic oracle the prophet presents God as disappointed with his people because of their iniquity. Nonetheless he predicted the eventual triumph of God's kingdom on earth:

It shall come to pass in the latter days
that the mountain of the house of the Lord
shall be established as the highest of the mountains,

and shall be raised above the hills;
and all the nations shall flow to it,
and many peoples shall come, and say:
'Come, let us go up to the mountain of the Lord,
to the house of the God of Jacob;
that he may teach us his ways
and that we may walk in his paths.'
For out of Zion shall go forth the law,
and the word of the Lord from Jerusalem.
He shall judge between the nations,
and shall decide for many peoples;
and they shall beat their swords into ploughshares,
and their spears into pruning hooks;
nation shall not lift up sword against nation,
neither shall they learn war any more. (Isaiah 2:2–4)

This future vision, however, is overshadowed by calamity. In chapter 2 Isaiah levelled criticism against idolatry, foretelling that such rebellion against God will bring about the destruction of the Temple. After discussing the place of Assyria in God's providential plan of devastation, Isaiah returned to the promise of salvation. A child will be born, he stated, who will be the Prince of Peace yet this promise is placed into the context of God's dissatisfaction with his people. According to the prophet, God will use Assyria as an instrument of punishment. Only a faithful remnant will remain, from which a redeemer will issue forth to bring about a new epoch in the nation's history:

There shall come forth a shoot from the stump of Jesse,
and a branch shall grow out of his roots.
And the Spirit of the Lord shall rest upon him ...
He shall not judge by what his eyes see,
or decide by what his ears hear;
but with righteousness he shall judge the poor,
and decide with equity for the meek of the earth; ...
The wolf shall dwell with the lamb,
and the leopard shall lie down with the kid,
and the calf and the lion and the fatling together.
(Isaiah 11:1–2, 3–4, 6)

In another passage, the prophet presented a song of praise which is to be sung on the day of Israel's redemption:

In that day this song will be sung in the land of Judah:
'We have a strong city;
he sets up salvation
as walls and bulwarks.
Open the gates,
that the righteous nation which keeps faith
may enter in.
Thou dost keep him in perfect peace,
whose mind is stayed on thee...
Trust in the Lord for ever,
for the Lord God is an everlasting rock.' (Isaiah 26:1–4)

A contemporary of Isaiah, the prophet Micah prophesied in the Southern Kingdom from 750 to 686 BCE. Condemning both Samaria and Judah for their wickedness, he declared that God will bring about judgment of the people: Samaria will be reunited and the places of idolatry destroyed. Yet despite this dire prediction, the prophet wished to reassure the nation that it would not be utterly cut off. God, he stated, has a purpose for them in the future:

I will surely gather all of you, O Jacob,
I will gather the remnant of Israel;
I will set them together
like sheep in a fold,
like a flock in its pasture,
a noisy multitude of men. (Micah 2:12)

Confident in the restoration of the people, he looked forward to an age of prosperity and fulfilment. Like Isaiah he predicted a time of messianic redemption. All nations, he declared, will go to the mountain of the Lord and dwell together in peace; in those days swords will be turned into ploughshares and each man will sit under his vine and fig tree:

For out of Zion shall go forth the law,
and the word of the Lord from Jerusalem.
He shall judge between many peoples,
and shall decide for strong nations afar off;
and they shall beat their swords into ploughshares,

and their spears into pruning hooks;
nation shall not lift up sword against nation,
neither shall they learn war any more;
but they shall sit every man under his vine and under
his fig tree,
and none shall make them afraid. (Micah 4:2–4)

The prophet Zephaniah was active in Judah during the reign of Josiah in about 625 BCE. Like the prophetic figures who preceded him, he warned against the nation's unfaithfulness: in his view, impending destruction would be the result of sinfulness. The great Day of the Lord is at hand, the prophet announced – it will be a time not of fulfilment but of calamity:

a day of distress and anguish,
a day of ruin and devastation,
a day of darkness and gloom,
a day of clouds and thick darkness,
a day of trumpet blast and battle cry
against the fortified cities
and against the lofty battlements. (Zephaniah 1:15–16)

Nothing will be able to prevent this outpouring of God's wrath; nonetheless, such devastation will not totally overwhelm the people. In the final part of his book, Zephaniah called on the Israelites to wait for God's vindication: he will gather the nations and pour out the heat of his anger. But at that time he will change the speech of all nations so that they will call on the name of the Lord and serve him with one accord. Knowing that their chastening is over, the people can exult. Certain of God's loving kindness, the nation can look forward to restoration and renewal. 'Sing aloud, O daughter of Zion,' he declared. 'Shout, O Israel! Rejoice and exult with all your heart, O daughter of Jerusalem' (Zephaniah 3:14). Confident of the future, the prophet declared in God's name:

'Behold, at the time I will deal
with all your oppressors.
And I will save the lame

and gather the outcast,
and I will change their shame into praise
and renown in all the earth.
At that time I will bring you home,
at the time when I gather you together;
yea, I will make you renowned and praised
among all the peoples of the earth,
when I restore your fortunes
before your eyes,' says the Lord. (Zephaniah 3:19–20)

In 626 BCE Jeremiah was commissioned as a prophet during the reign of Josiah – his ministry continued until the destruction of Judah. Jeremiah's earliest prophecies date from the time of Josiah: Judah, he stated, had forsaken God and in consequence will be punished. What is now required is repentance: if the inhabitants refuse, God will send forth an invader to subdue the country:

Flee for safety, O people of Benjamin,
from the midst of Jerusalem!
Blow the trumpet in Tekoa
and raise a signal on Beth-hac-cherem;
for evil looms out of the north. (Jeremiah 6:1)

Although persuaded that the country was doomed, Jeremiah was certain that the Lord will not completely destroy his people: a remnant will return with a new king at its head:

Behold, the days are coming, says the Lord, when I will raise up for David a righteous Branch, and he shall reign as king and deal wisely, and shall execute justice and righteousness in the land. In his days Judah will be saved, and Israel will dwell securely. (Jeremiah 23:5–6)

In his view, this new redemption will bring a new spiritual life for the Israelites. The Lord will create a new heart for his people and pour out a new spirit upon them:

Behold, the days are coming, says the Lord, when I will make a new covenant with the house of Israel and the house of Judah, not like the covenant which I made with their fathers when I took them by the hand to bring them out of the land of Egypt, my covenant which they broke, though I was their husband, says the Lord. But this is the covenant which I will make with the house of Israel after those days, says the Lord: I will put my law within them, and I will write it upon their hearts; and I will be their God, and they shall be my people. (Jeremiah 31:31–33)

For Jeremiah, in this blissful time a noble king filled with fear of the Lord will rule over the people:

Behold, the days are coming, says the Lord, when I will fulfil the promise I made to the house of Israel and the house of Judah. In those days and at that time I will cause a righteous Branch to spring forth for David; and he shall execute justice and righteousness in the land. In those days Judah will be saved and Jerusalem will dwell securely. And this is the name by which it will be called: 'The Lord is our righteousness.' (Jeremiah 33:14–16)

Post-exilic Prophecy

Dwelling in Babylon, the prophet Ezekiel began his ministry seven years before the conquest of Jerusalem. Like the earlier prophets, he castigated the Jewish people for their iniquity – because they had turned away from God further punishment will be inflicted upon them. Yet, despite the departure of God's glory from the Temple, Ezekiel reassured the nation that it will not be abandoned: 'Thus says the Lord God: I will gather you from the peoples, and assemble you out of the countries where you have been scattered, and I will give you the land of Israel' (Ezekiel 11:17).

In this spirit the prophet offered words of comfort and hope after the fall of Judah. In his view, God takes no pleasure in the death of sinners; what he requires instead is a contrite heart. Using the image of a shepherd and his flock, Ezekiel reassuringly declared that God will gather his people from exile and return them to the Promised Land:

For thus says the Lord God: Behold, I, I myself will search for my sheep, and will seek them out. As a shepherd seeks out his flock when some of his sheep have been scattered abroad, so

will I seek out my sheep; and I will rescue them from all places
where they have been scattered on a day of clouds and thick
darkness. (Ezekiel 34:11–12)

This prophecy is followed by a further vision of restoration – the Lord promises that cities will be reinhabited
and their ruins rebuilt. Such national restoration, the
prophet continued, will be accompanied by personal
dedication to the law. This reassurance was reinforced by
Ezekiel's vision of dry bones: although the nation had
been devastated, it will be renewed in a further deliverance:

As I prophesied, there was a noise, and behold, a rattling; and
the bones came together, bone to its bone. And as I looked,
there were sinews on them, and flesh had come upon them,
and skin had covered them ... Then he said to me, 'Son of
man, these bones are the whole house of Israel. Behold, they
say, "Our bones are dried up, and our hope is lost; we are
clean cut off." Therefore prophesy, and say to them, Thus
says the Lord God: Behold, I will open your graves, and raise
you from your graves, O my people; and I will bring you home
into the land of Israel ... And I will put my Spirit within you,
and you shall live, and I will place you in your own land ...'
(Ezekiel 37:7–8, 11, 14)

This vision is followed by a description of a future king
who will rule over his people. Under his dominion Jerusalem will benefit from the promises of the covenant:

My servant David shall be king over them; and they shall all
have one shepherd. They shall follow my ordinances and be
careful to observe my statutes. They shall dwell in the land
where your fathers dwelt that I gave to my servant Jacob; they
and their children and their children's children shall dwell
there for ever; and David my servant shall be their prince for
ever. (Ezekiel 37:24–25)

Like Ezekiel, Second Isaiah was anxious to offer words of
consolation to those who had experienced the destruction of Judah. In place of oracles of denunciation, the
prophet offered the promise of hope and restoration.
According to Second Isaiah, the Lord will return in
triumph to Jerusalem as a shepherd leading his flock: 'He

will feed his flock like a shepherd, he will gather the lambs in his arms, he will carry them in his bosom, and gently lead those that are with young' (Isaiah 40: 11). All the world will witness this act of deliverance and declare that the God of Israel is Lord.

In chapter 49 the prophet depicted the servant of the Lord through whom salvation will be brought to the ends of the earth – he will be mocked and despised. This theme is further developed in chapter 53:

> He was despised and rejected by men;
> a man of sorrows, and acquainted with grief;
> and as one from whom men hide their faces
> he was despised, and we esteemed him not.
> Surely he has borne our griefs
> and carried our sorrows;
> yet we esteemed him stricken,
> smitten by God, and afflicted.
> But he was wounded for our transgressions,
> he was bruised for our iniquities;
> upon him was the chastisement that made us whole,
> and with his stripes we are healed. (Isaiah 53:3–5)

Second Isaiah concluded with a vision of the future glory of Zion: God will be reunited with his people, and all will be fulfilled.

Echoing the predictions about the restoration of Zion in Second Isaiah, Third Isaiah emphasized the role of the Jewish people in God's providential plan. Through Israel's redemption all nations will be blessed, and the Temple will become a focus of worship for all peoples. Chapter 60 continues with a description of the glory of Zion. Jerusalem will be honoured throughout the world because of God's greatness. This theme is developed in the next chapter which speaks of a figure on whom the Spirit of God will rest; he will liberate all captives, bring tidings to the afflicted, and rebuild Zion:

> The Spirit of the Lord God is upon me,
> because the Lord has anointed me
> to bring good tidings to the afflicted;
> he has sent me to bind up the brokenhearted,

to proclaim liberty to the captives,
and the opening of the prison to those who are bound; ...
They shall build up the ancient ruins,
they shall raise up the former devastations;
they shall repair the ruined cities,
the devastations of many generations. (Isaiah 61:1, 4)

At this time Jerusalem will be acknowledged as the place where the Lord's redeemed dwell. Although God will judge those who have been unfaithful, the promise of restoration is offered to all who are loyal to him. Here Third Isaiah spoke of a new heaven and a new earth that will be created at the end of days:

'For behold, I create new heavens
and a new earth;
and the former things shall not be remembered
or come into mind.
But be glad and rejoice for ever
in that which I create;
for behold, I create Jerusalem a rejoicing,
and her people a joy ...
The wolf and the lamb shall feed together,
the lion shall eat straw like the ox;
and dust shall be the serpent's food.
They shall not hurt or destroy
in all my holy mountain.' (Isaiah 65: 17–18, 25)

The prophet Haggai, together with Zerubbabel, engaged in the rebuilding of the Temple. In a series of discourses he described the glories of the rebuilt Temple. God, he declared, is with his people. No longer is he determined that they should be punished because of their iniquities as he was when he used the Assyrians and Babylonians to accomplish his purposes. God, he stated, will be victorious over Israel's enemies. In this context, he emphasized that the Lord has chosen Zerubbabel as his servant – he is to be God's signet ring:

The word of the Lord came a second time to Haggai on the twenty-fourth day of the month, 'Speak to Zerubbabel, gover-nor of Judah, saying, I am about to shake the heavens and the earth, and to overthrow the throne of kingdoms; I am about to destroy the strength of the kingdoms of the nations, and overthrow the chariots and their riders; and the horses and their riders shall go down, every one by the sword of his fellow. On that day, says the Lord of hosts, I will take you, O Zerubbabel my servant, the son of She-alti-el, says the Lord, and make you like a signet ring; for I have chosen you, says the Lord of hosts.' (Haggai 2:20–23)

Zechariah, a contemporary of Haggai, also focused on the importance of rebuilding the Temple. Although the Lord had punished Judah by sending its inhabitants into exile for seventy years, the nation has suffered sufficiently. Now God's mercies will be made known to his chosen people – the land will prosper and God's dwelling will be established in Jerusalem. Prophesying about such a glorious future, Zechariah foretold that a king will come who will reign over the people. In a vision of hope, the prophet described this messianic figure who will be a descendant of David. He shall enter the city in triumph riding upon an ass: 'Rejoice greatly, O daughter of Zion! Shout aloud, O daughter of Jerusalem! Lo, your king comes to you; triumphant and victorious is he, humble and riding on an ass, on a colt the foal of an ass' (Zechariah 9:9).

According to Zechariah, God will redeem his people – he will strengthen them and bring them back to Zion; the inhabitants of Jerusalem shall be as though they had never been rejected:

I will signal for them and gather them in,
for I have redeemed them,
and they shall be as many as of old.
Though I scattered them among the nations,
yet in far countries they shall remember me,
and with their children they shall live and return.
(Zechariah 10:8–9)

Like Haggai and Zechariah, the prophet Malachi was a post-exilic prophet who was active after the exiles returned from Babylonia. In his view, Israel's sinfulness caused the Lord great distress. In order to remedy such transgression, God resolved to send his messenger to prepare the way for the Lord's entry into his Temple:

'Behold I send my messenger to prepare the way before me, and the Lord whom you seek will suddenly come to his temple; the messenger of the covenant in whom you delight; behold he is coming, says the Lord of hosts' (Malachi 3:1). However, because of their iniquity the people will not be able to deal with such a message – the coming of the Lord will thus not bring about Israel's redemption. Rather, it will be like a refiner's fire which will purify the nation.

The prophet insists that the promise of God's forgiveness and restoration will be fulfilled. Even though Israel has been iniquitous, God will return to his people if they seek him. In a final section of the book, Malachi described the Day of the Lord: it will be a time of destruction for the wicked and reward for those who fear his name. In conclusion Malachi announced that God will send the prophet Elijah before the Day of the Lord so that the nation will be reconciled:

> Behold, I will send you Elijah the prophet before the great and terrible day of the Lord comes. And he will turn the hearts of the fathers to their children and the hearts of children to their fathers, lest I come and smite the land with a curse. (Malachi 4:5–6)

The Psalms and Daniel

In addition to predictions about a future redemption of Israel found in the prophetic writings, the Book of Psalms contains numerous references to divine deliverance. The first of the messianic psalms begins with tumult. The world is in agitation – kings and princes have rebelled against God and his anointed. Yet, the Lord will prevail:

> He who sits in the heavens laughs;
> the Lord has them in derision.
> Then he will speak to them in his wrath,
> and terrify them in his fury, saying,
> 'I have set my king
> on Zion, my holy hill.'
> I will tell of the decree of the Lord:

> He said to me, 'You are my son,
> today I have begotten you.
> Ask of me, and I will make the nations your heritage,
> and the ends of the earth your possession.' (Psalm 2:4–8)

The allusion to the enthronement of the king is echoed in Psalm 110; here there is the same promise of victory over the enemies of the Lord:

> The Lord says to my lord:
> 'Sit at my right hand, till I make your enemies
> your footstool.'
> The Lord sends forth from Zion
> your mighty sceptre.
> Rule in the midst of your foes! (Psalm 110:1–2)

The subsequent verses promise defeat of Israel's enemies:

> He will execute judgment among the nations,
> filling them with corpses;
> he will shatter chiefs
> over the wide earth. (Psalm 110:6)

Other Psalms, traditionally attributed to King Solomon, present a different picture of this future king: he is the righteous ruler and the guarantee of the nation's prosperity:

> Give the king thy justice, O God,
> and thy righteousness to the royal son!
> May he judge thy people with righteousness,
> and thy poor with justice!
> Let the mountains bear prosperity for the people,
> and the hills, in righteousness!
> May he defend the cause of the poor of the people,
> give deliverance to the needy,
> and crush the oppressor! (Psalm 72:1–4)

For the Psalmist there is a fundamental link between the righteousness of the king and the fruitfulness of the land. Repeatedly the moral character of his rule is expressed:

> For he delivers the needy when he calls,
> the poor and him who has no helper.
> He has pity on the weak and the needy,

and saves the lives of the needy.
From oppression and violence he redeems their life;
and precious is their blood in his sight. (Psalm 72:112–14)

Continuing the theme of kingly rule, Psalm 21 states that the king is God's beloved whom he has given long life, victory, glory and majesty:

Thou has given him his heart's desire,
and has not withheld the request of his lips.
For thou dost meet him with goodly blessings;
thou dost set a crown of fine gold upon his head.
He asked life of thee; thou gavest it to him,
length of days for ever and ever.
His glory is great through thy help;
splendour and majesty thou dost bestow upon him.
Yea, thou dost make him most blessed for ever;
thou dost make him glad with the joy of thy presence.
(Psalm 21:2–6)

Connected with this notion of kingly rule, Psalm 132 contains God's promise to David that a scion of his dynasty will always reign in Israel:

The Lord swore to David a sure oath
from which he will not turn back:
'One of the sons of your body
I will set on your throne.
If your sons keep my covenant
and my testimonies which I shall teach them,
their sons also for ever
shall sit upon your throne.' (Psalm 132:11–12)

In summary then the Book of Psalms depicts the king as the Anointed of the Lord; he is placed by the Lord on his throne, proclaimed as his son, and appointed to maintain righteousness and justice throughout the land. Through his actions he conveys divine blessing to his people, fertility to the soil, and victory over foreign powers. Ruling over the entire world, his throne is established for all time.

Turning from the Psalms to the Book of Daniel, a different picture is given of such a divinely anointed deliverer. According to tradition, Daniel lived in Babylonia in the sixth century BCE during the final days of the Babylonian empire; most scholars, however, contend that the book was written in the second century BCE. Chapters 7 to 12 consist of a series of dreams foretelling future events. The first was a vision of beasts – a lion, a bear, a leopard and another creature terrifying in appearance. Each of these beasts symbolizes an empire: the lion corresponds to Babylonia; the bear the Medo-Persian empire; the leopard that of Alexander the Great; the fourth Rome. The theme is that Babylonia will be succeeded by these other empires until God's everlasting reign will be established. Here Daniel referred to one like the Son of Man who will be given dominion over all the earth:

> I saw in the night visions,
> and behold, with the clouds of heaven
> there came one like a son of man,
> and he came to the Ancient of Days
> and was presented before him.
> And to him was given dominion
> and glory and kingdom,
> that all peoples, nations, and languages
> should serve him;
> his dominion is an everlasting dominion,
> which shall not pass away,
> and his kingdom one
> that shall not be destroyed. (Daniel 7:13–14)

In the next vision a ram representing the Medo-Persian kings is succeeded by a goat – this denotes the king of the empire established by Alexander the Great. According to some scholars Daniel 8:23–25 refers to the coming of the Syrian King Antiochus IV, an enemy of the Jews: 'And at the latter end of their rule, when the transgressors have reached their full measure, a king of bold countenance, one who understands riddles, shall arise. His power shall be great, and he shall cause fearful destruction, and shall succeed in what he does, and destroy mighty men and the people of the saints.'

These visions are followed by Daniel's prayer for

deliverance despite the Israelites' sinfulness. Here Daniel appealed to God's mercy to deliver his people from their plight. In a response, Daniel was assured concerning the future of Jerusalem and the coming of the Anointed One:

> Seventy weeks of years are decreed concerning your people and your holy city, to finish the transgression, to put an end to sin, and to atone for iniquity, to bring in everlasting righteousness, to seal both vision and prophet, and to anoint a most holy place. Know therefore and understand that from the going forth of the word to restore and build Jerusalem to the coming of an anointed one, a prince, there shall be seven weeks. (Daniel 9:24–25)

This supplication is followed in chapter 10 by a vision of the last days. On the twenty-fourth day of the first month, a man clothed in linen whose loins were girded with rich gold of Uphaz appeared on the Tigris. In a series of speeches, he strengthened and encouraged Daniel, revealing to him later kings who would reign during the period of Greek rule. This passage is followed by prophecies concerning an unknown king, and a final assurance that the Lord will remain faithful to his people:

> And there shall be a time of trouble, such as never has been since there was a nation till that time; but at that time your people shall be delivered, every one whose name shall be found written in the book. And many of those who sleep in the dust of the earth shall awake, some to everlasting life, and some to shame and everlasting contempt. And those who are wise shall shine like the brightness of the firmament; and those who turn many to righteousness, like the stars for ever and ever. (Daniel 12:1–3)

2

The Messiah in the Apocrypha and Pseudepigrapha

The Apocrypha consists of Jewish works written during the Second Temple period. Because many of them were composed during the prosperous years of the Hasmonean dynasty, they do not contain the despair which was evinced by the destruction of Jerusalem. Hence these books are not dominated by the hope of messianic deliverance. Nonetheless, the concept of a future redemption was not forgotten, and there are frequent references to the ingathering of the exiles. In addition, several of these works describe a future world in which the righteous will be rewarded. The Pseudepigrapha, on the other hand, date from a later period after the devastation of Jerusalem and the Temple and are filled with messianic portrayals. Here the Day of Judgment and the birth pangs of the Messiah are described in detail; further, the personality of the Messiah as well as the Days of the Messiah are depicted in vivid terms. The Pseudepigrapha themselves are divided into two types: the Palestinian Pseudepigraphical books were composed for the most part in Jerusalem in the Hebrew language – those containing the most important messianic references consist of the *Book of Enoch*, *Jubilees*, the *Psalms of Solomon*, the *Assumption of Moses*, the *Syriac Book of Baruch*, and *Fourth Ezra*. The Hellenistic Pseudepigrapha were composed largely in Alexandria in Greek: the text in which messianic expectations play an important role are the *Sibylline Oracles*. Although the messianic predictions in these writings vary considerably, they bear witness to the deep longing of the nation for divine deliverance and redemption during this tumultuous period of Jewish history.

The Apocrypha

Throughout *Ben Sira* (c. 190–170 BCE) the love of Israel is manifest; in the author's view, Israel is pre-eminent among the nations. Such dedication is manifest even when he is discussing abstract ideas. Hence in chapter 35 while discussing the plight of the oppressed, he turns to God's chosen people:

> Yea, the Lord will not tarry
> And the mighty One will not refrain himself
> Till he smite the loins of the merciless,
> And requite vengeance (to the arrogant);
> Till he dispossess the sceptre of pride,
> And the staff of wickedness is utterly cut down;
> Till he redeem to man his due,
> And recompense people according to their devising,
> Till he plead the cause of his people,
> And rejoice them with salvation. (*Ben Sira* 35:22–25)

The next chapter makes it clear that this vision is of the Age to Come. This prayer of hope is filled with messianic expectation:

> Save us, O God of all,
> And cast thy fear upon all the nations.
> Shake thy hand against the strange people,
> And let them see thy power.
> As thou has sanctified thyself in us before them,
> So glorify thyself in them before us;
> That they may know, as we also know,
> That there is none other God but thee.
> Renew the signs, and repeat the wonders,
> Make Hand and Right Arm glorious.
> Waken indignation and pour out wrath,
> Subdue the foe and expel the enemy.
> Hasten the 'end' and ordain 'the appointed time' ...
> Gather all the tribes of Jacob,
> That they may receive their inheritance as in the days of old.
> Compassionate the people that is called by thy name,

Israel, whom thou didst surname Firstborn.
Compassionate thy holy city,
Jerusalem, the place of thy dwelling.
Fill Sion with thy majesty,
And thy temple with thy glory ...
That all the ends of the earth may know
That thou art the eternal God. (*Ben Sira* 36:1–22)

Here this passage outlines the various stages of messianic anticipation – the destruction of Israel's enemies, the sanctification of God's name by elevating the Jewish nation, the performance of miracles, the ingathering of the exiles, the glorification of Jerusalem and the Temple, reward for the righteous and punishment for the wicked, and the fulfilment of prophetic expectations.

Although *Ben Sira* does not specify that redemption will come through Davidic rule or an individual Messiah, the author does specify that the house of David will be preserved. As a reward for his accomplishments, God gave him the decree of the kingdom and established his throne over Jerusalem (*Ben Sira* 47:11). Later in the same chapter he adds:

Nevertheless God did not forsake his mercy,
Nor did he suffer any of his words to fall to the ground.
He will not cut off the posterity of his chosen,
Nor will he destroy the offspring of them that love him.
And he will give to Jacob a remnant,
And to the house of David a root from him. (*Ben Sira* 47:22)

Just as the kingdom of David will last for ever, so will the priesthood of Aaron:

And he exalted a holy one (like unto him),
Even Aaron of the tribe of Levi.
And he made him an eternal ordinance,
And bestowed upon him his majesty. (*Ben Sira* 45:6–7)

Thus, not only does he believe in the continuation of the house of David, but also in the perpetuity of the priesthood of Aaron. In another passage, both of these institutions are coupled together:

Therefore for him, too, he established an ordinance,

A covenant of peace to maintain the sanctuary:
that to him and to his seed should appertain
The High-Priesthood for ever.
Also his covenant was with David,
The son of Jesse, of the tribe of Judah;
The inheritance of the king is his son's alone,
While the inheritance of Aaron (belongs) to him and to his
seed. (*Ben Sira* 45:24–25)

In *Ben Sira* there is a further future expectation – the
coming of Elijah in the messianic age. After describing the
mighty deeds of the prophet, he adds:

Who art ready for the time, as it is written,
To still wrath before the fierce anger of God,
To turn the heart of the fathers unto the children,
And to restore the tribes of Israel. (*Ben Sira* 48:10)

For Ben Sira, not only will the Jewish people endure for all
time, but they will be a light to the gentiles. Speaking of
Abraham and his descendants, the author declares:

Therefore with an oath he promised him
To bless the nations in his seed,
To multiply him 'as the dust of the earth',
And to exalt his seed 'as the stars';
To cause them to inherit 'from sea to sea
And from the River to the ends of the earth'.
(*Ben Sira* 44:21)

Turning to the *Apocryphal Baruch* (early part c. 130 BCE;
later part c. 90 BCE), in the first part of this work there is a
reference to the idea that God will bring about the return
of the exiles to the land of their fathers once they have
turned from their evil ways (*Baruch* 2:24–35). Later in the
book the author describes Jerusalem which is to be
renewed:

O Jerusalem, look about thee toward the east,
And behold the joy that cometh unto thee from God.
Lo, thy sons come, whom thou sentest away,
They come gathered together from the east to the west (at
the word of the Holy One),
Rejoicing in the glory of God.

Put off, O Jerusalem, the garment of thy mourning and affliction,
And put on the comeliness of the glory that cometh from God for ever.
Cast about thee the robe of the righteousness which cometh from God;
Set a diadem on thine head of the glory of the Everlasting.
For God will show thy brightness unto every region under heaven.
For thy name shall be called of God for ever
The peace of righteousness, and the glory of godliness.
(*Baruch*: 4:36–5:4)

The book continues with a description of the return of the exiles:

Arise, O Jerusalem, and stand upon the height,
And look about thee toward the east,
And behold thy children gathered from the going down of the sun unto the rising thereof (at the word of the Holy One),
Rejoicing that God hath remembered them.
For they went from thee on foot,
Being led away of their enemies:
But God bringeth them in unto thee
Borne on high with glory, as on a royal throne.
For God hath appointed that every high mountain, and the everlasting hills, should be made low,
That Israel may go safely in the glory of God.
Moreover the woods and every sweet-smelling tree have overshadowed Israel (by the commandment of God).
For God shall lead Israel with joy in the light of his glory
With the mercy and righteousness that cometh from him.
(*Baruch* 5:5–9)

Alluding to Second Isaiah's vision of the ingathering of the exiles, the author depicts the re-establishment of Zion in glowing terms.

Unlike earlier apocryphal works which predict the transformation of earthly life, *II Maccabees* (c. 70 BCE) speculates about the nature of eternal life. Here the author emphasizes that reward and punishment are to be meted out in a future world. Of particular importance is a passage, presumably critical of Sadducean doctrine, stating that Judas Maccabeus was 'bearing in mind the resurrection – for if he had not expected the fallen to rise again, it would have been superfluous and silly to pray for the dead' (*II Maccabees* 12:43–44). Here the resurrection of the dead is conceived in bodily terms. Elsewhere the author contends that only the righteous will be restored to life; for sinners like Antiochus Epiphanes there is no deliverance from death.

Finally like *II Maccabees*, the *Wisdom of Solomon* is preoccupied with the World to Come, eternal life, and divine retribution. Thus in chapter 3 the author describes the reward for the righteous:

> But the souls of the righteous are in the hand of God,
> and no torment shall touch them.
> In the eyes of fools they seemed to die;
> And their departure was accounted to be their hurt,
> And their going from us to be their ruin:
> But they are in peace.
> For though in the sight of men they be punished,
> Their hope is full of immortality. (*Wisdom of Solomon* 3:1–4)

Turning to the destruction of the wicked, he describes the future Day of the Lord:

> He shall sharpen stern wrath for a sword:
> And the world shall go forth with him to fight against
> his insensate foes,
> Shafts of lightning shall fly with true aim,
> And from the clouds, as from a well drawn bow, shall
> they leap to the mark.
> And as from an engine of war shall be hurled hailstones
> full of wrath;
> The water of the sea shall rage against them,
> And rivers shall sternly overwhelm them;
> A mighty blast shall encounter them,
> And as a tempest shall it winnow them away:
> So shall lawlessness make all the land desolate,
> And their evil-doing shall overturn the thrones of princes.
> (*Wisdom of Solomon* 5:20–23)

The Ethiopic Book of Enoch

Although the early parts of the *Ethiopic Book of Enoch* date from c. 110 BCE, its later parts in all probability were composed after the destruction of the Temple. Here the author presents a variety of reflections about the messianic age beginning with the Day of Judgment. During this period the Day of the Lord was identified with the 'birth pangs of the Messiah' – this did not refer to any suffering of the Messiah himself, but to the tribulations of the messianic age. In the *Book of Enoch* these events are portrayed in dramatic terms. The Holy Lord will come forth from his dwelling, appear from the highest of heavens and tread on Mount Sinai. As a consequence men will be overcome with fear and anguish will spread through the world. The mountains will be shaken, the high hills made low, and the earth sink; everyone will then undergo judgment. The righteous will be rewarded, whereas the wicked will be punished for their deeds (*Enoch* 1:3–9).

Not only will the wicked be chastised, so too will Satan and the angels who have corrupted the earth be brought to judgment. In addition, evil spirits, demons and devils will be condemned. The righteous, however, will prosper:

> Then shall they rejoice with joy and be glad,
> And into the holy place shall they enter;
> And its fragrance shall be in their bones,
> And they shall live a long life on earth,
> Such as their fathers lived:
> And in their days shall no sorrow or plague
> Or torment of calamity touch them. (*Enoch* 25:6)

In other passages the destruction which is to be visited upon the world is described in detail: severe affliction will come upon the world: the destitute will abandon their children, pregnant women will miscarry, and mothers will cast sucklings away:

> In those days the nations shall be stirred up,
> And the families of the nations shall arise on the day of destruction.

And in those days the destitute shall go forth and carry off
their children,
And they shall abandon them, so that their children shall
perish through them:
Yea, they shall abandon their children (that are still)
sucklings, and not return to them,
And shall have no pity on their beloved ones. (*Enoch* 99:4–5)

On those days fathers and sons will be slain in one place;
and brothers will fall together:

And in those days in one place the fathers together with
their sons shall be smitten
And brothers one with another shall fall in death
Till the streams flow with their blood. (*Enoch* 100:1)

As far as the messianic age is concerned, the *Book of Enoch*
states that only the elect will be worthy of entering the
divine realm. They will live and never sin again, and there
will be light and knowledge for the worthy:

And then there shall be bestowed upon the elect wisdom,
And they shall all live and never again sin ...
And they shall not again transgress,
Nor shall they sin all the days of their life,
Nor shall they die of (the divine) anger or wrath,
But they shall complete the number of the days of their life.
(*Enoch* 5:8–9)

As far as the terrestrial messianic expectations are concerned, at the end of days the righteous will be delivered,
beget a thousand children, and complete all their days in
peace. The whole earth will be filled with righteousness
and the fields will prosper. Along with such material
prosperity, the *Book of Enoch* describes the spiritual
renewal that will take place during the Days of the
Messiah. The Lord will open the storehouses of heavenly
blessing which he will pour out upon the faithful:

And in those days I will open the store chambers of blessing
which are in the heaven, so as to spread them down upon
the earth over the work and labour of the children of men.
And truth and peace shall be associated together
throughout all the days of the world and throughout all the
generations of men. (*Enoch* 11:1–2)

In the historical section of the book, the author presents the history of the world and the Jewish people to the present day – all of this is a prelude to the Days of the Messiah. Like the author of the Book of Daniel, historical characters take the form of various creatures. After surveying the rise and fall of empires, the author goes on to describe the Day of Judgment which is followed by the Days of the Messiah. The Messiah, he states, is a 'white bull with large horns', and all the beasts of the field and birds of the air fear and make supplications to him.

Added to this conception of the messianic age is a detailed description of the Messiah in chapters 37–71. Here it is asserted that the Messiah existed before the creation of the world. His dwelling place is under the wings of the God of Spirits where the elect shall pass before him:

> And in that place mine eyes saw the Elect One of
> righteousness and of faith,
> And I saw his dwelling-place under the wings of the Lord of
> Spirits.
> And righteousness shall prevail in his days,
> And the righteous and elect shall be without number before
> him for ever and ever.
> And all the righteous and elect before him shall be strong as
> fiery lights,
> And their mouth shall be full of blessing. (*Enoch* 39:6–7)

On that day the Elect One will sit on the throne of glory and choose the occupations of men and their dwelling-places; their spirits will grow strong when they see the Messiah, and heaven and earth will be transformed. The elect will then dwell in a new and blessed earth upon which sinners and evildoers will not set foot:

> On that day Mine Elect One shall sit on the throne of glory
> And shall try their works,
> And their places of rest shall be innumerable.
> And their souls shall glory strong within them when they see
> mine elect ones,
> And those who have called upon My glorious name:
> Then will I cause Mine Elect One to dwell among them.

And I will transform the heavens and make it an eternal
blessing and light:
And I will transform the earth and make it a blessing:
And I will cause mine elect ones to dwell upon it:
But the sinners and evil-doers shall not set foot thereon.
(*Enoch* 45:3–5)

The next chapter begins with imagery drawn from the
Book of Daniel:

And I asked the angel who went with me and showed me all
the hidden things, concerning that Son of Man, who he was,
and whence he was, (and) why he went with the Head of
Days? And he answered and said unto me:

This is the Son of Man who hath righteousness,
With whom dwelleth righteousness,
and who revealeth all the treasures of that which is hidden,
Because the Lord of Spirits hath chosen him,
And whose lot hath the pre-eminence before the Lord of
Spirits in uprightness for ever.
And this Son of Man whom thou hast seen
Shall raise up the kings and the mighty from their seats
(And the strong from their thrones)
And shall loosen the reins of the strong,
And break the teeth of the sinners. (*Enoch* 46:2–4)

In chapter 47 the Ancient of Days is depicted on the
throne of glory where the books of the living will be
opened before him:

In those days I saw the Head of Days when he seated himself
upon the throne of his glory,
and the books of the living were opened before him:
And all his host which is in heaven above and his counsellors
stood before him,
And the hearts of the holy were filled with joy. (*Enoch* 47:3)

In the next sections the importance of the Messiah is
emphasized. He will be a staff to the righteous and holy,
and a light to the gentiles. All who dwell on earth will
worship and bless him and praise the God of Spirits.
During the Days of the Messiah wisdom will be like the
waters that cover the sea, and the glory of the Lord will be
revealed. At this time drastic changes will take place in

nature. The earth will bring to life those who have died and the Messiah will choose from among those who have risen the righteous and holy: he will sit upon his throne and reveal secret knowledge:

> And in those days the earth shall also give back that which has been entrusted to it,
> And Sheol also shall give back that which it has received,
> And hell shall give back that which it owes.
> For in those days the Elect One shall arise,
> And he shall choose the righteous and holy from among them:
> For the day has drawn nigh that they should be saved.
> (*Enoch* 51:1–2)

The latter part of the book adds new features to the presentation of the Messiah and his relation to the righteous. All the heavenly powers praise the Elect One; he will be seated on the throne of glory as he judges the deeds of the holy:

> And the Lord of Spirits placed the Elect One on the throne of glory.
> And he shall judge all the works of the holy above in the heavens,
> and in the balance shall their deeds be weighed.
> (*Enoch* 61:8)

Then God commands the mighty kings and exalted rulers to recognize the Elect One as they see him seated on the throne with the spirit of righteousness poured out upon him:

> And he will summon all the host of the heavens, and all the holy ones above, and the host of God, the Cherubim, Seraphim and Ophannim, and all the angels of power, and all the angels of principalities, and the Elect One, and the other powers on the earth (and) over the water. On that day shall raise one voice, and bless and glorify and exalt in the spirit of faith, and in the spirit of wisdom, and in the spirit of patience, and in the spirit of mercy, and in the spirit of judgment and

of peace, and in the spirit of goodness, and shall all say with one voice: 'Blessed is he, and may the name of the Lord of Spirits be blessed for ever and ever.' (*Enoch* 61:10–11)

On this day the righteous and elect will be saved; the God of Spirits will abide over them and with the Son of Man they will eat and lie down and rise up forever:

And the Lord of Spirits will abide over them.
And with that Son of Man shall they eat
And lie down and rise up for ever and ever.
And they shall have been clothed with garments of glory,
And these shall be the garments of life from the Lord of Spirits:
and your garments shall not grow old,
Nor your glory pass away before the Lord of Spirits.
(*Enoch* 62:14–16)

Jubilees, Testaments of the Twelve Patriarchs, and Psalms of Solomon

Written in c. 100–90 BCE, the *Book of Jubilees* does not refer to a King-Messiah – in all likelihood this omission was due to the fact that at the time of its composition there existed an anointed king and priest of the house of Levi. Nonetheless, the book does contain messianic ideas similar to what is found in the Apocrypha. Because of the nation's sinfulness, the people will be punished; this will be followed by repentance, and only then will Israel will be redeemed. The Lord will build his sanctuary in their midst and dwell among them:

And I will build my sanctuary in their midst, and I will dwell with them, and I will be their God and they shall be my people in truth and righteousness. (*Jubilees* 1:18)

Then a new world will be made: heaven and earth and all creatures will be renewed and the sanctuary of the Lord will be manifest in Jerusalem on Mount Zion.

In chapter 23 the process of redemption is described in

detail. After fearful punishment, there will be complete repentance and then divine redemption:

> And all their days they shall complete and live in peace and joy,
> And there shall be no Satan nor any evil destroyer;
> For all their days shall be days of blessing and healing.
> And at that time the Lord will heal his servants,
> And they shall rise up and see great peace,
> And drive out their adversaries.
> And the righteous will see and be thankful,
> And rejoice with joy for ever and ever,
> And shall see all their judgments and their curses on their enemies. (*Jubilees* 23: 29–30)

The *Testaments of the Twelve Patriarchs* (c. 110–70 BCE) consists of ethical injunctions preceded by stories about the tribal patriarchs. In the last section of the Testament of Simeon there is a lofty messianic oracle. Here Simeon encourages his sons to remove their envy and stiff-neckedness. Then, he states:

> As a rose shall my bones flourish in Israel,
> And as a lily my flesh in Jacob,
> And my odour shall be as the odour of Libanus;
> And as cedars shall holy ones be multiplied from me for ever,
> and their branches shall stretch afar off.
> Then shall perish the seed of Canaan,
> And a remnant shall not be unto Amelek,
> And all the Cappadocians shall perish,
> And all the Hittites shall be utterly destroyed.
> Then shall fail the land of Ham
> And all the people shall perish.
> Then shall all the earth rest from trouble
> And all the world under heaven from war.
> Then the Mighty One of Israel shall glorify Shem,
> For the Lord God shall appear on earth,
> And Himself save men.
> (*Testaments of the Twelve Patriarchs* 6:2–5)

Again, in the Testament of Levi, there is a depiction of

divine redemption. After punishment has come from the Lord, he will raise up to the priestly office a new priest to whom all the words of God will be revealed; he will then execute judgment upon the earth:

> Then shall the Lord raise up a new priest.
> And to him all the words of the Lord shall be revealed;
> And he shall execute a righteous judgment upon the earth
> for a multitude of days
> And his star shall arise in heaven as of a king.
> Lighting up the light of knowledge as the sun the day.
> And he shall be magnified in the world.
> He shall shine forth as the sun on the earth,
> And shall remove all darkness from under heaven,
> And there shall be peace in all the earth.
> The heavens shall exult in his days,
> And the earth shall be glad
> And the clouds shall rejoice;
> (And the knowledge of the Lord shall be poured upon the
> earth, as the waters of the seas;)
> And the angels of the glory of the presence of the Lord shall
> be glad in him.
> The heavens shall be opened,
> And from the temple of glory shall come upon him
> sanctification. (*Testaments of the Twelve Patriarchs* 18:2–6)

The Testament of Judah also contains a vivid description of messianic redemption. The star of peace will arise and walk in meekness among men. The heavens will be opened and pour out their blessings. The spirit of truth will come upon the children of Judah. A shoot will come forth from the stock of Judah and the rod of righteousness will be in his hand to judge and save all those who call upon him. All the tribes will become one people and have one language. Those who died in grief will arise and awake to everlasting life. The hungry will be satisfied, the poor made rich, and the weak become strong:

> And ye shall be the people of the Lord, and have one
> tongue;
> And there shall be no spirit of deceit of Beliar,

For he shall be cast into the fire for ever.
And they who have died in grief shall arise in joy,
And they who were poor for the Lord's sake shall be made rich,
And they who are put to death for the Lord's sake shall awake to life. (*Testaments of the Twelve Patriarchs* 25:3–4)

The *Psalms of Solomon* is a later book written in c. 45 BCE which enlarges on the personality of the Messiah. According to the author, the Hasmonean kings had acted wickedly; therefore it is a mistake to regard them as Messiahs. Turning to God, he prays for redemption which he connects with the ingathering of the exiles:

Turn, O God, thy mercy upon us, and have pity upon us;
Gather together the dispersed of Israel, with mercy and goodness;
For thy faithfulness is with us.
And (though) we have stiffened our neck, yet thou art our chastener;
Overlook us not, O our God, lest the nations swallow us up, as though there were none to deliver.
(*Psalms of Solomon* 8:33–36)

Such messianic predictions continue in *Psalm* 11:

Blow ye in Zion on the trumpet to summon the saints,
Cause ye to be heard in Jerusalem the voice of him that bringeth good tidings;
For God hath had pity on Israel in visiting them.
Stand on the height, O Jerusalem, and behold thy children,
From the East and the West, gathered together by the Lord;
From the North they come in the gladness of their God,
From the isles afar off God hath gathered them.
High mountains hath he abased into a plain for them;
The hills fled at their entrance ...
Put on, O Jerusalem, thy glorious garments;
Make ready thy holy robe;
For God hath spoken good concerning Israel, for ever and ever. (*Psalms of Solomon* 11:1–6, 8)

Continuing this messianic theme, *Psalm* 17 contains an

accusation against the Hasmonean dynasty followed by a depiction of the redeemer of Israel:

> Behold, O Lord, and raise up unto them their king, the son of David,
>
> At the time in the which thou seest, O God, that he may reign over Israel thy servant.
>
> And gird him with strength, that he may shatter unrighteous rulers,
>
> And that he may purge Jerusalem from nations that trample (her) down to destruction ...
>
> And he shall gather together a holy people, whom he shall lead in righteousness,
>
> And he shall judge the tribes of the people that has been sanctified by the Lord his God ...
>
> And he shall have the heathen nations to serve him under his yoke:
>
> And he shall glorify the Lord in a place to be seen of all the earth;
>
> And he shall purge Jerusalem, making it holy as of old:
>
> So that nations shall come from the ends of the earth to see his glory,
>
> Bringing as gifts her sons who had fainted,
>
> And to see the glory of the Lord, wherewith God hath glorified her.
>
> And he (shall be) a righteous king, taught of God, over them,
>
> And there shall be no unrighteousness in his days in their midst,
>
> For all shall be holy and their king the anointed of the Lord ...
>
> He (will be) shepherding the flock of the Lord faithfully and righteously,
>
> And will suffer none among them to stumble in their pasture.
>
> He will lead them arights,
>
> And there will be no pride among them that any among them should be oppressed.
>
> This (will be) the majesty of the king of Israel whom God knoweth;
>
> He will raise him up over the house of Israel to correct him.
>
> His words (shall be) more refined than costly gold, the choicest;

In the assemblies he will judge the peoples, the tribes of the
sanctified.
His words (shall be) like the words of the holy ones in the
midst of sanctified peoples.
Blessed be they that shall be in those days,
In that they shall see the good fortune of Israel which God
shall bring to pass in the gathering together of the tribes.
(*Psalms of Solomon* 17:23–24; 28; 32–36; 45–50)

Assumption of Moses, Syriac Book of Baruch, Fourth Book of Ezra, and the Sibylline Oracles

Dating from c. 4–6 CE the *Assumption of Moses* does not
contain an account of the Messiah; nonetheless in chapter
10 there is a depiction of the Day of the Lord. According
to the author, Israel will triumph over her enemies, and
there will be bliss and freedom in the Age to Come:

And then his kingdom shall appear throughout all his
creation,
And then Satan shall be no more,
And sorrow shall depart with him.
Then the hands of the angel shall be filled
Who has been appointed chief,
And he shall forthwith avenge them of their enemies.
For the Heavenly One will arise from his royal throne,
And he will go forth from his holy habitation
With indignation and wrath on account of his sons ...
For the Most High will arise, the Eternal God alone,
And he will appear to punish the gentiles,
And he will destroy all their idols.
Then thou, O Israel, shalt be happy,
And thou shalt mount upon the necks and wings of the
eagle,
And they shall be ended.
And God will exalt thee,
And he will cause thee to approach to the heaven of the
stars,
In the place of their habitation.
And thou shalt look from on high and shalt see thy enemies
(in Gehenna).
And thou shalt recognize them and rejoice,

And thou shalt give thanks and confess thy
Creator.(*Assumption of Moses* 10:1–3; 7–10)

Dating from c. 70–80 CE the *Syriac Book of Baruch* contains
numerous messianic expectations beginning with the
birth pangs of the Messiah. The appointed time is coming
– it will be a period of affliction:

Behold! the days come
And it shall be when the time of the age has ripened,
And the harvest of the seed of the good and the evil has
come,
That the Mighty One will bring upon the earth,
And upon its inhabitants and its rulers,
Perturbation of spirit and anxiety of mind.
And they shall hate one another,
And provoke one another to fight;
And the mean shall rule over the honourable,
And those of low degree shall be extolled above the famous.
And the many shall be delivered into the hands of few,
And those who were nothing shall rule over the strong;
And the poor shall have control over the rich,
And the impious shall exalt themselves above the heroic.
And the wise shall be silent,
And the foolish shall speak. (*Syriac Book of Baruch* 48: 53–4)

These events are to be followed by the coming of the
Messiah. After the signs have appeared, the Messiah will
appear and he shall rule in peace and glory:

And then healing shall descend in dew,
And disease shall withdraw,
And anxiety and anguish and lamentation pass from
amongst men,
And gladness proceed through the whole earth.
And no one shall again die untimely,
Nor shall any adversity suddenly befall.
And judgements and revilings, and contentions, and
revenges,
And blood, and passions, and envy, and hatred,
And whatsoever things are like these
shall go into condemnation when they are removed ...
And wild beasts shall come from the forest
and minister unto men,

And asps and vipers shall come forth from their holes
to submit themselves to a little child.
And women shall no longer then
have pain when they bear,
Nor shall they suffer torment
when they yield the fruit of the womb ...
For that time is the consummation of that which is
corruptible,
And the beginning of that which is not corruptible.
Therefore those things which were predicted
shall belong to it;
Therefore it is far away from evils,
And near to those things which die not.
(*Syriac Book of Baruch* 73:2–74:3)

Central to the *Syriac Book of Baruch* is the notion of a new
world which is different from the messianic age. This is
the World to Come, a new era in which there is no end
and the righteous will receive a great light:

And the hour comes which abides forever,
And the new world, which does not turn to corruption
those who enter into its blessedness,
And has no mercy on those who depart to torment,
And leads not to perdition those who live in it.
(*Syriac Book of Baruch* 44:12)

The *Fourth Book of Ezra* which dates from c. 90–100 CE
contains numerous messianic expectations along similar
lines. Here, too, are descriptions of the birth pangs of the
Messiah. According to the *Fourth Book of Ezra*, the signs
that will precede the coming of the Messiah include great
confusion and desolation. Responding to the question
when such signs will take place, Ezra receives new signs
indicating that the end is near:

When in the world there shall appear
quakings of places
tumult of peoples,
schemings of nations,
confusion of leaders,
disquietude of princes,
then shalt thou understand that it is of these things the Most
High has spoken since the days that were aforetime from the

beginning. For just as with respect to all that has happened in the world, the beginning (?) is obscure, but the end (issue) manifest, so also are the times of the Most High: the beginnings are (visible) in portents and secret signs, and the end in effects and marvels. (*Fourth Book of Ezra* 8:62–9:6)

These occurrences are followed by the messianic age and the Day of Judgment. After the signs of the Messiah:

My son the Messiah shall be revealed, together with those who are with him, and shall rejoice the survivors four hundred years. And it shall be, after these years, that my Son the Messiah shall die, and all in whom there is human breath. Then shall the world be turned into the primaeval silence seven days, like as at the first beginnings, so that no man is left. And it shall be after seven days that the Age which is not yet awake shall be roused, and that which is corruptible shall perish. And
the earth shall restore those that sleep in her,
and the dust those that are at rest therein,
(and the chambers shall restore those that were committed unto them). (*Fourth Book of Ezra* 7:26–32)

The end of the world and the beginning of the World to Come is initiated by the Day of Judgment. Then

the Most High shall be revealed
upon the throne of judgement:
(and then cometh the End)
and compassion shall pass away,
(and pity be far off,)
and longsuffering withdrawn;
But judgement alone shall remain,
truth shall stand,
and faithfulness triumph.
And recompense shall follow,
and the reward be made manifest;
Deeds of righteousness shall awake,
and deeds of iniquity shall not sleep.
and then shall the pit of torment appear,
and over against it the place of refreshment;
The furnace of Gehenna shall be made manifest,
and over against it the Paradise of delight.
(*Fourth Book of Ezra* 7:33–36)

In a series of messianic visions, the personality and work of the Messiah are depicted. From before the creation of the world he existed, and he is being kept with God until the time for him to be revealed. He is as strong as a lion and swift as an eagle, able to dominate all those who seek to wage war against him.

Finally, the *Sibylline Oracles* whose contents date from c. 140 BCE–130 CE, contain a variety of messianic ideas. Book III describes the confrontation between God and the anti-Messiah Beliar; here the Lord is victorious, bringing about the transformation of nature:

> From the stock of Sebaste Beliar shall come in later time and shall raise the mountain heights and raise the sea, the great fiery sun and the bright moon, and he shall raise up the dead and shall perform many signs for men: but they shall not be effective in him. Nay, but he deceives mortals, and many shall he deceive, Hebrews faithful and elect and lawless too, and other men who have never yet listened to the word of God. But at whatsoever time the threatened vengeance of the Almighty God draws near, and fiery energy comes through the swelling surge to earth, and burns up Beliar and the overweening men, even all who have put their trust in him, then the world shall be under the domination of a woman's hands obeying her every behest. Then when a widow shall reign over the whole world and cast both gold and silver into the godlike deep, and the brass and iron of shortlived man cast into the sea, then the elements of the world one and all shall be widowed, what time God Whose dwelling is in the sky shall roll up the heaven as a book is rolled. And the whole firmament in its varied forms shall fall on the divine earth and on the sea: and then shall flow a ceaseless cataract of raging fire, and shall burn land and sea, and the firmament of heaven and the stars and creation itself it shall cast into one molten mass and clean dissolve. (*Sibylline Oracles*, Book III, 63–87)

Reversing the order of other works, the *Sibylline Oracles* depicts the war with Gog and Magog after the advent of the messianic age. Then the children of Israel will dwell on their own soil with the King-Messiah ruling over them. He will put an end to all wars on the earth and make a covenant with the righteous. After the war, all the sons of God will live quietly around the Temple, rejoicing in their salvation. Then all the peoples will see God's mercies and turn to him. They will acknowledge the rightness of the commandments and forsake their idols. Then humanity will live in peace:

> But when the fated day shall reach this consummation. . . . Earth the universal mother shall give to mortals her best fruit in countless store of corn, wine and oil. Yea, from heaven shall come a sweet draught of luscious honey, the trees shall yield their proper fruits, and rich flocks, and kine and lambs of sheep and kids of goats. . . . No war shall there be any more nor drought throughout the land, no famine nor hail to work havoc on the crops. But there shall be a great peace throughout all the earth. (*Sibylline Oracles*, Book III, 741–55)

Then all the earth will be filled with knowledge of God; famine will cease, wars will be ended, and one system of law will prevail for all.

3

The Rabbinic View

Once the Temple had been destroyed and the Jewish people driven out of their homeland, the nation was bereft. In their despair the ancient Israelites longed for a kingly figure who would deliver them from exile and rebuild their holy city. Drawing on messianic ideas found in Scripture, the Apocrypha and Pseudepigrapha, they foresaw the coming of a future deliverance when all peoples would be converted to the worship of the one true God. Such conceptions animated rabbinic speculation about the eschatological unfolding of history when God would intervene on behalf of Jewry. According to a number of early rabbinic sages, such a process of redemption would be brought about through charity, repentance and the observance of Jewish law. Nevertheless, prior to the coming of such messianic deliverance, the world would be subject to serious tribulations defined as 'the birth pangs of the Messiah'. These would be followed by the arrival of Elijah, the forerunner of the Messiah. Subsequently a second figure – the Messiah ben Joseph – would engage in conflict with Gog and Magog, the enemies of the Israelites. Although he would be killed in battle, the King-Messiah (Messiah ben David) would eventually be victorious, and with his coming the dispersion of Israel would cease. All exiles would be returned to Zion, and earthly life would be totally transformed. Finally at the end of this messianic period, all human beings would undergo judgment and either be rewarded with heavenly bliss or punished everlastingly. This vision of a future hope was animated by the Jewish conviction that God would not abandon the Jews to exile; the promise of messianic redemption and return to Israel served as a basis for overcoming the nation's despondency at losing the Holy Land and the people's sacred institutions.

The Coming of the Messiah

As time passed, rabbinic scholars elaborated the themes found in Scripture as well as in Jewish literature of the Second Temple period. In midrashic collections and the Talmud they formulated a complex eschatological scheme divided into a series of stages. According to a number of sages, messianic deliverance will be brought about by charity, repentance and the observance of the law. Hence Rabbi Jose stated: 'Great is charity, in that it brings the redemption nearer, as it is said: (Isaiah 56:1), "Thus saith the Lord, Keep ye justice and do charity; for my salvation is near to come, and my favour to be revealed"' (*Baba Bathra* 10a). Again, Rabbi Jose the Galilean declared: 'Great is repentance, because it brings near redemption, as it is said (Isaiah 59:20), "And a redeemer will come to Zion, and unto them that turn from transgression in Jacob." Why will a redeemer come to Zion? Because of those that turn from transgression in Jacob' (*Yoma* 86b).

Given such conditions, the Messiah will come in power and glory, yet he would be preceded by numerous travails. As in the Pseudepigrapha, such sufferings are referred to in rabbinic literature as 'the birth pangs of the Messiah'. Thus the Talmud states:

> With the footprints of the Messiah, insolence will increase and death reach its height; the vine will yield its fruit but the wine will be costly. There will be none to offer reproof, and the whole empire will be converted to heresy. The meeting place of scholars will be laid waste and Gablan be made desolate; and the people of the frontier will go about from city to city with none to take pity on them. The wisdom of the Scribes will become foolish, and they that shun sin will be despised. The young will insult their elders, and the great will wait upon the insignificant. (*Sanhedrin* 97a)

Other passages from the School of Akiva depict the prevalence of iniquity as a prelude to the messianic age. In this regard Rabbi Nehemiah said: 'In the generation when the son of David comes, impudence will increase and esteem will be perverted; the vine will yield its fruit but the wine will be costly; and the whole empire will be converted to heresy, with none to offer rebuke' (*Sanhedrin* 97a).

Again, Rabbi Judah said:

In the generation when the son of David comes, the meeting-place of scholars will be given over to harlotry. Galilee will be laid waste and Gablan be made desolate; and the people of the frontier will go about from city to city with none to take pity on them. The wisdom of the Scribes will become foolish, and they that shun sin will be despised. The face of this generation is as the face of a dog, and truth is lacking, as it is written (Isaiah 59:15): 'And truth shall be lacking, and he that departeth from evil maketh himself a prey.' (*Sanhedrin* 97a).

According to Rabbi Nehorai, the young will grow increasingly insolent: 'In the generation when the son of David comes, the young will insult their elders, and the elders will wait upon the young: "the daughter riseth up against her mother, the daughter-in-law against her mother-in-law"; and the face of this generation is as the face of a dog; and a son does not feel ashamed before his father' (*Sanhedrin* 97a).

Finally, Simeon ben Yohai depicted the devastation accompanying the coming of the Messiah:

In the week when the son of David comes, in the first year this verse will be fulfilled: 'I will cause it to rain upon one city, and cause it not to rain upon another city' (Amos 4:7). In the second year the arrows of hunger will be sent forth. In the third a great famine: men, women and children will die; pious men and saints (will be few), and the Law will be forgotten by its students. In the fourth, partial plenty. In the fifth, great plenty, when men will eat, drink and be merry, and the Law will return to its students. In the sixth, voices. In the seventh,

wars; and at the end of the seventh year, the son of David will
come. (*Sanhedrin* 97a)

Not only will these natural disasters come upon the land,
the word of the Lord will also be forgotten during the
time of messianic travail. As the Talmud states:

> When our teachers entered the vineyard (school) at Yabneh,
> they said: The Torah is destined to be forgotten in Israel, as it
> is written (Amos 8:11): 'Behold, the days come, saith the Lord
> God, that I will send a famine in the land, not a famine of
> bread, nor a thirst for water, but of hearing the words of the
> Lord.' It is further written (Amos 8:12): 'And they shall
> wander from sea to sea, and from the north even to the east;
> they shall run to and fro to seek the word of the Lord, and
> shall not find it.' – 'The word of the Lord' means *Halakhah*;
> 'the word of the Lord' means The End; 'the word of the
> Lord' means prophecy. (*Shabbat* 138b)

Despite these dire predictions, the rabbis maintained that
the prophet Elijah will return prior to the coming of the
Messiah to solve all earthly problems. An illustration of
this belief is found in the Talmud where the word '*Teku*' is
used whenever a religious question cannot be resolved.
Literally this term means 'let it remain unresolved'; however, this expression was interpreted as signifying that the
Tishbite (Elijah) will resolve all difficulties and problems.
Hence the Talmud indicates that Elijah is expected to
solve difficult legal problems, yet he would not come on
the Sabbath or a festival because his presence might
disturb their preparations:

> If the fourteenth (of *Nisan*) falls on the Sabbath, everything
> (that is leavened) must be removed before the Sabbath; and
> heave-offerings, whether unclean, or doubtful, or clean must
> be burnt ... This is the ruling of Rabbi Judah ben Eliezer of
> Bartotha, which he stated in the name of Rabbi Joshua. But
> they said to him: 'Clean heave-offerings should not be burnt,
> lest persons be found who need to eat them (before the
> Passover).' ... He retorted: 'Then on your reasoning even
> those in doubt should not be burnt, lest Elijah come and
> declare them clean.' They said to him: 'It has long been
> assured to Israel that Elijah will come neither on the eve of

the Sabbath nor on the eve of festivals on account of the trouble.' (*Pesahim* 13a)

Further, Elijah's role in the messianic era will be to certify the ritual uncleanliness of families which suffered from mixed marriages or forbidden unions, and also grant permission to hitherto excluded peoples from marrying Jews. Moreover, Elijah's task will be to bring back to the Jewish people those who had been wrongfully excluded from the community. All this is to be done in anticipation of the coming of the Messiah. This is the meaning of a classic passage in the Talmud which depicts his mission:

> Rabbi Joshua said: I have received a tradition from Rabban Johanan ben Zakkai, who heard from his teacher, and his teacher from his teacher, as a *halakhah* given to Moses from Sinai, that Elijah will come not to declare unclean or clean (families in general), to remove afar or bring nigh (in general), but to remove afar those (families) that were removed afar by force. The family of Beth-Zerepha was in the land beyond Jordan, and the sons of Zion removed it afar by force. And yet another (family) was there, and the sons of Zion brought it nigh by force. The like of these Elijah will come to declare unclean or clean, to remove afar or to bring nigh. Rabbi Judah (ben Bathyra) says: To bring nigh but not to remove afar. Rabbi Ishmael says: To bring agreement where there is a matter for dispute. And the Sages say: Neither to remove afar nor to bring nigh, but to make peace with the world, as it is written (Malachi 4:5): 'Behold I will send you Elijah the prophet . . . And he shall turn the heart of the fathers to the children, and the heart of the children to their fathers.' (*Eduyyoth* 8:7)

As a forerunner of the Messiah, Elijah will announce from the top of Mount Carmel his coming; it will be the King-Messiah of Israel who will initiate the end of history and the advent of God's Kingdom on earth.

Messiah ben Joseph and Messiah ben David

Drawing on earlier conceptions, the rabbis formulated the doctrine of a second Messiah – the son of Joseph – who would precede the King-Messiah, the Messiah ben

David. According to legend, this Messiah would engage in battle with Gog and Magog, the traditional enemies of Israel, and be slain. Only after this defeat would the Messiah ben David arrive in glory. As a hero, the Messiah ben Joseph will be mourned by the Jewish people. As the Talmud states:

> And the land shall mourn, every family apart; the family of the house of David apart, and their wives apart (Zechariah 12:12) ... What is the cause of this mourning. Rabbi Dosa and our teachers differ on the point. One said, The cause is the slaying of Messiah ben Joseph, and another said, The cause is the slaying of the evil inclination. It is well with him who said the cause is the slaying of Messiah ben Joseph, for that agrees with the verse (Zechariah 12:10), 'And they shall look upon him who they have pierced, and they shall mourn for him as one mourneth for his only son.' (*Sukkah* 52a)

In this final struggle against the nation's enemies, God will himself act on behalf of Israel. Thus in the *midrash*, the rabbis maintain that:

> There are four shinings forth: the first was in Egypt, as it is written (Psalm 80:1), 'Give ear, O Shepherd of Israel, thou that leadest Joseph like a flock, thou that art enthroned upon the cherubim, shine forth'; the second was at the time of the giving of the Law, as it is written (Deuteronomy 33:2), 'He shone forth from Mount Paran'; the third will take place in the days of Gog and Magog, as it is written (Psalm 94:1), 'Thou God to whom vengeance belongeth, shine forth'; the fourth will be in the days of the Messiah (ben David) as it is written (Psalm 50:2), 'Out of Zion, the perfection of beauty, shall God shine forth.' (*Siphre*, Deut. 343)

Regarding this struggle, the rabbis speculated that God had already revealed the defeat of Gog and Magog to Moses. Hence Rabbi Nehemiah stated that in Numbers 11:26 Eldad and Medad prophesied concerning this battle:

> As it is written (Ezekiel 38:17), 'Thus saith the Lord God: Art thou he of whom I spoke in old time by my servants the prophets of Israel, that prophesied in those days (from many) years that I would bring thee against them?' and so on. Read

not *shanim* (years) but *shnayim* (two). And which two prophets prophesied the same thing at the same time? Eldad and Medad, of course. (*Sanhedrin* 17a)

According to Simeon ben Yohai, the war with Gog and Magog was one of the most terrible evils to befall humankind:

> Viciousness in a man's own household is worse that the war with Gog and Magog. For it is said (Psalm 3:1), 'A Psalm of David, when he fled from Absalom his son'; and next it is written (Psalm 3:1), 'Lord, how many are mine adversaries become! Many are they that rise up against me.' Now in regard to the war with Gog and Magog it is written (Psalm 2:1), 'Why are the nations in an uproar? And why do the peoples mutter in vain?' – but it is not written, 'How many are mine adversaries become!' (*Berakhoth* 7b)

Yet after Israel is delivered from this struggle, the King-Messiah will come to bring about the actual messianic Kingdom on earth.

During the early rabbinic period, numerous legends emerged about the names and personality of this glorious figure. In their speculations about the nature of the Messiah ben David, scholars applied various titles to him. Rabbi Jose the Galilean for example stated: 'The Messiah's name is called Peace, for it is written (Isaiah 9:6), "Everlasting Father, Prince (called) Peace"' (Klausner, 1956, 462). Another name of the Messiah was Hadrach, as Rabbi Judah explained: 'In the land of Hadrach and in Damascus shall be his resting place, for the Lord's is the eye of man and all the tribes of Israel (Zechariah 9:1). This (the name Hadrach) is the Messiah, who will be *Had* ("sharp") toward the nations of the world, but *Rach* ("soft") toward Israel' (*Siphre*, Deut. 1). Again, in the Talmud the Messiah is depicted as having several titles: 'The School of Shila said: His name is Shiloh ... The School of Rabbi Yannai said: His name is Yinnon ... The School of Rabbi Haninah maintained: His name is Haninah' (*Sanhedrin* 98b). In such cases these schools chose a name resembling their name or head. Other names had symbolic significance: hence the Messiah is called the

'Comforter' on the basis of Lamentations 1:16: 'Because the comforter is far from me, even he that should refresh my soul' (*Sanhedrin* 98b).

Turning to the nature of the King-Messiah, the early sages focused on his exalted and moral character. According to one *Baraitha*, he already existed in paradise: 'Nine persons entered into paradise during their lifetime: Enoch son of Jared, Elijah, the Messiah, Eliezer the servant of Abraham, Hiram king of Tyre, Ebedmelech the Ethiopian, Jabez son of Rabbi Judah the patriarch, Bithiah daughter of Pharaoh, and Serah daughter of Asher' (*Derekh Erets Zuta*, end of ch. I). Concerning his characteristics, Rabbi Tanhum stressed his spiritual integrity:

> Bar Kappara expounded in Sepphoris: Why is it written (Ruth 3:17) 'These six measures of barley gave he to me'? ... He (Boaz) symbolically intimated to her (Ruth) that six sons were destined to come forth from her, who should each be blessed with six blessings: David, Messiah, Daniel, Hananiah, Mishael, and Azariah ... (Concerning the Messiah) it is written (Isaiah 11:2): 'And the spirit of the Lord shall rest upon him, the spirit of wisdom and understanding, the spirit of counsel and might, the spirit of knowledge and the fear of the Lord.' (*Sanhedrin* 93ab)

With the coming of the Messiah ben David, the dispersion of Israel will cease; all exiles will return from the four corners of the earth to the Holy Land. Thus Simeon ben Yohai proclaimed:

> Come and see how beloved is Israel before the Holy One, blessed is he; for wherever they went into exile the *Shekinah* (God's presence) was with them. They went into exile in Egypt, and the *Shekinah* was with them, as it is written (1 Samuel 2:27), 'Did I indeed reveal myself unto the house of thy father when they were in Egypt?' They went into exile in Babylonia, and the *Shekinah* was with them, as it is written (Isaiah 43:14), 'For your sake I was sent to Babylonia.' Likewise, when they shall be redeemed in the future, the *Shekinah* will be with them, as it is written (Deuteronomy 30:3), 'Then the Lord thy God will return with thy captivity'. It does not say 'will bring back thy captivity' but 'will return

with thy captivity' – teaching that the Holy One. blessed is he,
returns with them from the places of exile. (*Megillah* 29a)

Here God is described as accompanying his chosen
people in exile, sharing their sufferings. Yet with the
messianic redemption, the exiles will return to Zion in
triumph with God at their head. Clouds of glory shall be
spread over them, and they will come singing with joy on
their lips.

The Messianic Age and Heaven

Rabbinic literature contains frequent speculation about
the Days of the Messiah (also referred to as 'The World to
Come'). Thus the Talmud describes how the land will be
divided:

> And the division in the world to come will not be like the
> division in this world. In this world, should a man possess a
> cornfield, he does not possess an orchard; should he possess
> an orchard he does not possess a cornfield. But in the world
> to come, there will be no single individual who will not
> possess land in mountain, lowland, and valley; for it is said
> (Ezekiel 48:31), 'the gate of Reuben, one; the gate of Judah,
> one; the gate of Levi, one' (that is, all the tribes will have
> equal possessions). (*Baba Bathra* 122a)

In their depictions of the messianic age, Jewish sages
stressed that the Days of the Messiah will be totally
different from the present world. Concerning the fruitfulness of the harvest, for example, they stressed that his era
'is not like this world. In this world there is the trouble of
harvesting and treading (grapes); but in the world to
come a man will bring one grape on a wagon or in a ship,
put it in the corner of his house, and use its contents as if
it had been a large wine cask ... There will be no grape
that will not contain thirty kegs of wine (Klausner, 1956,
410).

Speculating on the length of this period, the rabbis
differed as to its duration. Rabbi Eliezer, for instance,
stated: 'The Days of the Messiah will be forty years; for it is
written in one place (Deuteronomy 8:3), "And he afflicted

thee, and suffered thee to hunger and fed thee with manna", and in another place it is written (Psalm 90:15), "Make us glad according to the days wherein thou hast afflicted us according to the years wherein we have seen evil."' Rabbi Dosa said: 'Four hundred years; for it is written in one place (Genesis 15:13), "And they shall serve them, and they shall afflict them four hundred years"; and in another place it is written (Psalm 90:15), "Make us glad according to the days wherein thou has afflicted us."' Rabbi Jose the Galilean said: 'Three hundred and sixty-five years, according to the number of days in the solar year, as it is written (Isaiah 63:4), "For the day of vengeance was in my heart, and my year of redemption has come"' (*Sanhedrin* 99a).

According to another *Baraitha*: 'It was taught in the school of Elijah: The world will endure six thousand years: two thousand in chaos, two thousand under the Law, and two thousand during the messianic age; but because of our many iniquities time has been lost from the last period (that is, four thousand years have already passed, yet the Messiah has not yet arrived)' (*Sanhedrin* 97ab).

Again another passage relates:

> Rab Hanan bar Tahlifa sent this word to Rab Joseph: I met a man who had a scroll written in the Assyrian character and in the holy language. I said to him, 'Where did you get this?' He said to me, 'I hired myself as a mercenary in the Persian (Roman) army, and I found it among the secret archives of Persia (Rome).' In it is written: 'Four thousand two hundred and ninety-one years after its creation, the world will be orphaned. As to the years which follow, some of them will witness the wars of the dragons, some the wars of Gog, and Magog, and the rest will be the messianic age, and the Holy One, blessed be he, will not renew his world until after seven thousand years.' (*Sanhedrin* 97b)

Other traditions, however, assert that such reckoning is fruitless. Hence the Talmud records: 'Seven things are hidden from men. These are the day of death, the day of consolation, the depth of judgment, no man knows what is in the mind of his friend; no man knows which of his business ventures will be profitable, or when the kingdom of the house of David will be restored or when the sinful kingdom will fall' (*Pesahim* 54b).

Despite such disagreement about the length of this period, there was a general acceptance among the sages that at the end of the Days of the Messiah, all would be changed. At the close of this era, a final judgment would come upon all humankind. Yet for such judging to take place, all those who had died will need to be resurrected. Given that there is no explicit belief in eternal salvation in the Bible, the rabbis of the post-biblical period were faced with the difficulty of proving that the doctrine of resurrection of the dead is contained in Scripture which they regarded as authoritative. To do this, they employed a number of principles of exegesis based on the assumption that each word in the Pentateuch was transmitted by God to Moses.

Thus, for example, Rabbi Eliezer, the son of Rabbi Jose, claimed to have refuted the Sectarians who maintained that resurrection is not a biblical doctrine: 'I said to them: You have falsified your Torah ... For ye maintain that resurrection is not a biblical doctrine, but it is written (Numbers 15:31ff), "Because he hath despised the word of the Lord, and hath broken his commandments, that soul shall utterly be cut off, his iniquity shall be upon him." Now, seeing that he shall utterly be cut off in this world, when shall his iniquity be upon him? Surely in the next world' (*Sanhedrin* 90b).

Again, Rabbi Meir asked:

> Whence do we know resurrection from the Torah? From the verse, 'Then shall Moses and the children of Israel sing this song unto the Lord' (Exodus 15:1). Not 'sang', but 'sing' is written. Since Moses and the children of Israel did not sing a second time in this life, the text must mean that they will sing after resurrection. Likewise it is written, 'Then shall Joshua build an altar unto the Lord God of Israel' (Joshua 8:30). Not 'build' but 'shall build' is stated. Thus resurrection is intimated in the Torah' (*Sanhedrin* 91b).

Similarly, Rabbi Joshua ben Levi said: 'Whence is resurrection derived from the Torah? From the verse, "Blessed are they that dwell in thy house, they shall ever praise thee" (Psalm 84:4). The text does not say "praised thee" but "shall praise thee". Thus we learn resurrection from the Torah' (*Sanhedrin* 91b).

The principal qualification for divine reward is obedience to God's law; those who are judged righteous will enter into Heaven (*Gan Eden*) which is portrayed in various ways in rabbinic sources. One of the earliest descriptions portrays its nature:

> The *Gan Eden* at the east measures 800,000 years (at ten miles per day or 3650 miles per year). There are five chambers for various classes of the righteous. The first is built of cedar, with a ceiling of transparent crystal. This is the habitation of non-Jews who become true and devoted converts to Judaism. They are headed by Obadiah the prophet and Onkelos the proselyte, who teach them the Law. The second is built of cedar, with a ceiling of fine silver. This is the habitation of the penitents, headed by Manasseh, king of Israel, who teaches them the Law.
>
> The third chamber is built of silver and gold, ornamented with pearls. It is very spacious, and contains the best of heaven and of earth, with spices, fragrance, and sweet odours. In the centre of this chamber stands the Tree of Life, 500 years high. Under its shadow rest Abraham, Isaac, and Jacob, the tribes, those of the Egyptian exodus, and those who died in the wilderness, headed by Moses and Aaron. There are also David and Solomon, crowned and Chileab, as if living, attending on his father, David. Every generation of Israel is represented except that of Absalom and his confederates. Moses teaches them the Law, and Aaron gives instruction to the priests.
>
> The Tree of Life is like a ladder on which the souls of the righteous may ascend and descend. In a conclave above are seated the Patriarchs, the Ten Martyrs, and those who sacrificed their lives for the cause of his sacred Name. These souls descend daily to the *Gan Eden* to join their families and tribes, where they lounge on soft cathedras studded with jewels. Everyone, according to his excellence, is received in audience to praise and thank the ever-living God; and all enjoy the brilliant light of the *Shekinah*. The flaming sword, changing from intense heat to icy cold, and from ice to glowing coals,

guards the entrance against living mortals. The size of the sword is ten years. The souls on entering paradise are bathed in the 248 rivulets of balsam and attar.

The fourth chamber is made of olive-wood and is inhabited by those who have suffered for the sake of their religion. Olives typify bitterness in taste and brilliancy in light (olive oil), symbolizing persecution and its reward. The fifth chamber is built of precious stones, gold and silver, surrounded by myrrh and aloes. In front of the chamber runs the river Gihon, on whose banks are planted shrubs affording perfume and aromatic incense. There are couches of gold and silver and fine drapery. This chamber is inhabited by the Messiah ben David, Elijah and the Messiah of Ephraim (Joseph). In the centre are a canopy made of the cedars of Lebanon, in the style of the tabernacle, with posts and vessels of silver; and a settee of Lebanon wood with pillars of silver and a seat of gold, the covering thereof of purple. (A. Super, 1967, 191–3)

Punishment for the Wicked

As with Heaven, Jewish sources contain extensive and elaborate descriptions of Hell. In rabbinic literature the word usually used for Hell is *Gehinnom*, originally a valley near Jerusalem where Moloch was worshipped because of its biblical connection with the netherworld. This identification was reinforced by the rabbinic view that one of the three gates of Hell is located in Jerusalem. According to one rabbinic tradition, God created Hell on the second day along with the firmament, fire and the angels. For this reason, God could not say of this day as of the others that he 'saw that it was good'. In another rabbinic tradition, on the other hand, Hell is described as pre-existent, created two thousand years before Heaven and Earth.

When God decided to create the cosmos, the Torah (the Jewish tradition personified) was sceptical about the value of an earthly world because of the sinfulness of human beings. God, however, dispelled her doubts by assuring her that sinners would have the opportunity of mending their ways, and that Hell was created to punish those who would not repent. The punishment of the wicked in Hell follows the biblical principle of 'measure for measure' which is enunciated in the *Mishnah*. In general, fire was the punishment for those sinners who committed incest, murder and idolatry or cursed their parents and teachers. Other sins that merit Hell are ·adultery, idolatry, pride, mockery, hypocrisy and anger as well as following the advice of one's wife, instructing an unworthy pupil, and speaking in an unseemly fashion. Through repentance one could escape the torments of Hell, but this was not the only way; the sages of the Talmud produced a list of exemptions which restricted the number of sinners condemned to punishment. Those who during their lives suffered from grinding poverty, from painful and odious bowel diseases, from the persecution of the Romans or from a bad wife were excluded. In addition, giving charity to the poor, teaching Torah to the son of an ignoramus, visiting the sick, eating three meals on the Sabbath, and saying the Shema regularly and devoutly help protect one from from the fires of *Gehinnom*.

We know that Hell is very hot, because when God visited Abraham after he was circumcised, God bored a hole in Hell so that its heat might reach the earth, thereby preventing any wayfarer from venturing abroad on the highways and disturbing Abraham in his pain. According to the *midrash*, Isaac was alarmed by seeing Hell at the feet of Esau. Scarcely had he entered the house when its walls began to get hot because of the nearness of Hell which Esau brought with him. The rabbis also stated that the springs of Tiberius are hot because its waters pass the gates of Hell. Other sources portray the coldness of Hell. For example, the angels who guided Enoch through Heaven told him that God had prepared a terrible place for sinners in the northern regions of the third heaven where there was fire as well as cold and ice on all sides.

In another rabbinic source, fire is located in a southern chamber of Hell next to a cave of smoke. The wind blowing from this direction brings heat and sultriness; were it not for the winged angel which keeps the south wind back with his pinions, the world would be consumed. These fires of Hell are reflected in the evening twilight. According to the Talmud, the sun passes paradise in the morning and Hell in the evening. Thus, just as dawn reflects the roses of paradise, so the evening twilight reflects the fires of Hell. In another passage God tells Elijah that the four phenomena (wind, earthquake, fire and a still small voice) represent the worlds through which man must pass; fire presenting the tribunal in Hell. In another passage Hell is described, not as a place of light and fire, but dark with impenetrable gloom as thick as a coin.

For the rabbis, the entry to Hell is through three gates. The entrance is guarded over by a special angel, Dumah, who announces the arrival of newcomers to the nether-world. He takes the souls of the wicked and casts them down into the depths of Sheol. This is repeated every week at the close of the Sabbath, since during the day of rest the souls are released from their torment but must return as the Sabbath ends.

As to Hell itself, it is described as having seven divisions. In the Talmud Rabbi Joshua ben Levi deduced the divisions of Hell from biblical quotations: *she'ol, abadon, be'er shahat, bor sha'on, tit ha-yawen, zel mawet* and *erez ha-tahtit*. This talmudic concept of the sevenfold structure of Hell is elaborated in midrashic sources. According to one source it requires 300 years to traverse the height or width or the depth of each division, and it would take 6300 years to go over a tract of land equal in extent to the seven divisions. Each of these seven divisions of Hell is in turn divided into seven subdivisions and in each compartment there are seven rivers of fire, and seven of hail. The width of each is 1000 ells, its depth 1000, and its length 300; they flow from each other and are supervised by the angels of destruction. Besides, in each compartment there are 7000 caves, and in each cave there are 7000 crevices, and in every crevice there are 7000 scorpions. Every scorpion has 300 rings, and in every ring 7000 pouches of venom from which flow seven rivers of deadly poison. If a man handles it, he immediately bursts, every limb is torn from his body, his bowels are cleft, and he falls upon his face.

Confinement to Hell is the result of disobeying God's Torah as is illustrated by the *midrash* concerning the evening visit of the soul to Hell before it is implanted in an individual. There it sees the angels of destruction smiting with fiery scourges; the sinners all the while are crying out, but no mercy is shown to them. The angel guides the soul and then asks: 'Do you know who these are?' Unable to respond, the soul listens as the angel continues: 'Those who are consumed with fire were created like you. When they were put into the world, they did not observe God's Torah and his commandments. Therefore they have come to this disgrace which you see them suffer. Know your destiny is also to depart from the world. Be just, therefore, and not wicked, that you may gain the future world.'

The soul was not alone in being able to see Hell; a number of biblical personages entered into its midst. Moses, for example, was guided through Hell by an angel, and his journey there gives us the most complete picture of its torments:

> When Moses and the angel of Hell entered Hell together, they saw men being tortured by the angels of destruction. Some sinners were suspended by their hair and their breasts by chains of fire. Such punishments were inflicted on the basis of the sins that were committed: those who hung by their eyes had looked lustfully upon their neighbour's wives and possessions; those who hung by their ears had listened to empty and vain speech and did not listen to the Torah; those who hung by their tongues had spoken foolishly and slanderously; those who hung by their hands had robbed and murdered their neighbours. The women who hung by their hair and breasts had uncovered them in the presence of young men in order to seduce them. (Ginzberg, 1968, Vol. II, 310–13)

In another place, *Alukah*, Moses saw sinners suspended by their feet with their heads downward, and their bodies covered with long black worms. These sinners were punished in this way because they swore falsely, profaned the Sabbath and the holy days, despised the sages, called their neighbours by unseemly nicknames, wronged the orphan and the widow, and bore false witness.

In another section Moses saw sinners prone on their faces with 2000 scorpions lashing, stinging and tormenting them. Each of these scorpions had 70,000 stings, and each 70,000 pouches of poison and venom. So great was the pain they inflicted that the eyes of the sinners melted in their sockets. These sinners were punished in this way because they had robbed other Jews, were arrogant in the community, put their neighbours to shame in public, delivered their fellow Jews into the hands of gentiles, denied the Torah, and maintained that God is not the creator of the world.

In another place, *Tit ha-Yawen*, sinners stood in mud up to their navels while angels of destruction lashed them with fiery chains, and broke their teeth with fiery stones. These sinners were punished because they had eaten forbidden food, lent their money at usury, wrote the name of God on amulets of gentiles, used false weights, stole money from fellow Jews, ate on the Day of Atonement, and drank blood. Finally, after visualizing these tortures, Moses saw how sinners were burnt in the section of Hell called *Abaddon*. There one half of their bodies was immersed in fire; the other half was placed in snow while worms bred in their own flesh crawled over them. At the same time the angels of destruction beat them without ceasing. Secretly these sinners put snow in their armpits to relieve the pain. These sinners were punished in this fashion because they had committed incest, murder, idolatry, called themselves gods, and cursed their parents and teachers.

This eschatological scheme in which Hell played a fundamental role was formulated over the centuries by innumerable rabbis and should not be seen as a flight of fancy. Rather it was a serious attempt to make sense of God's ways. Israel was God's chosen people; the nation had been driven from their homeland. Yet the Messiah would come to deliver them from exile and redeem the world. The period of messianic redemption would unfold in various stages, culminating in a final judgment with reward for the righteous and punishment for the wicked; in this way the vindication of the righteous was assured in the Hereafter.

4

Jesus the Messiah

From the Gospels, it appears that a Jewish sect of Christians emerged in the first century BCE. In consonance with messianic expectations of this period, these believers expected their Messiah to bring about the fulfilment of human history. According to the New Testament, Jesus of Nazareth spent most of his life in Galilee where he preached the coming of the Kingdom of God. After a brief association with John the Baptist, he attracted disciples from among the most marginalized sectors of society to whom he proclaimed this message. Despite his popularity among the masses, he soon aroused suspicion and hostility from both Jewish and Roman officials and was put to death during the reign of Pontius Pilate in about 30 CE. Afterwards his followers believed he had risen from the dead, appeared to them, and promised to return to usher in the period of messianic rule. The Jewish community, however, rejected these claims; in their view, Jesus did not fulfil the messianic role as outlined in Scripture and portrayed in rabbinic sources. Despite the growth of the Christian community in the years after Jesus death, Jews continued to wait for the advent of a Messiah-King who would return the exiles to Zion, resurrect the dead, and usher in a period of messianic redemption.

Jesus

Although little is known of Jesus' early life, it appears that he received a traditional Jewish education. According to Luke 4:16–20, he was deemed worthy to read the Torah in the synagogue in Nazareth. Luke also provides an account of Jesus' pilgrimage to Jerusalem when he was twelve; he had gone there to participate in one of the Jewish festivals. When his parents found him in the Temple, he asked: 'Did you not know that I must be in my Father's house?' (Luke 2:49), implying that he had a special sense of religious vocation.

Nearly twenty years elapsed between these early stories and Mark's depiction of Jesus' encounter with his cousin, John the Baptist. Residing in the Judean desert, John lived a simple life, dressing in camel's hair and eating only locusts and honey. Claiming to be a messenger of the Lord, he sought to bring the good news of a new society that was about to commence (Luke 3:2–3). Calling on the Jewish nation to prepare themselves to meet God, he predicted the coming of the Messiah (Luke 3:7–17).

When Jesus came to his cousin to be baptized, John initially did not want him to participate in this symbol of repentance. Yet at Jesus' insistence, he relented. It was at this point that Jesus began to understand his mission. According to Mark, he heard the words: 'Thou art my beloved Son; with thee I am well pleased' (Mark 1:11). This appears to be an allusion to Psalm 2:7 ('You are my son, today I have begotten you') which had come to take on messianic overtones as well as the suffering servant in Isaiah 42:1 ('my chosen, in whom my soul delights'). Thus at his baptism, it appears that Jesus was reassured of his own spiritual relationship with God and reminded of his role as God's promised deliverer.

After his baptism, Jesus was faced with a series of temptations. First he was challenged with the temptation to improve society economically by turning stones into bread (Luke 4:1–4); the second temptation was to throw himself down from the tower of the Temple without injuring himself in order to demonstrate his Messiahship (Luke 4:9–12); finally, he was tempted to become a political Messiah and reign over the world. Instead, however, Jesus sought to fulfil God's word as the long-awaited redeemer of humanity.

In embarking on this mission, Jesus undertook several roles. He was pre-eminently God's Messiah. In Mark, the earliest Gospel, Jesus only once referred to himself in this way (Mark 9:41) – nonetheless, on four other occasions, his followers called him Messiah, and he apparently accepted the title. In Matthew, Peter declared: 'You are the Christ'; in response, Jesus stated that Peter was blessed to have had such an insight (Matthew 16:16–17). Again, in his trial before the leaders of the Jewish nation, Jesus acknowledged to the High Priest that he was the Messiah (Mark 14:61–62). Further, in the story of Jesus' healing a person possessed by demons, Jesus allowed the man to address him as 'Son of the Most High God', and he instructed him to return to his family and tell them what the Lord had done (Mark 5:1–20). On another occasion, Jesus had set out for Jericho when a blind beggar, Bartimaeus, addressed him as 'Son of David'. Though some of those who heard him told him to remain silent, Jesus did not join them, implying that he had accepted this title (Mark 10:46–52). From these four instances, it is clear that although Jesus believed he was the Messiah, he did not wish to make this claim himself since his understanding of his messianic role differed from traditional expectations. For the Jews the Messiah was to be a political king, but for Jesus being the Messiah involved humble service and obedience.

Another title applied to Jesus in the Gospels is 'Son of Man'. In Mark Jesus spoke of 'the Son of Man coming in clouds with great power and glory' (Mark 13:26); in Luke he states that the Son of Man will be 'seated at the right hand of the power of God' (Luke 22:69). In these two cases, there is an explicit reference to Daniel where the Son of Man is depicted in supernatural terms: 'one like a son of man, and he came to the Ancient of Days and was presented before him. And to him was given dominion and glory and kingdom, that all peoples, nations and languages should serve him; his dominion is an everlasting dominion, which shall not pass away, and his kingdom one that shall not be destroyed' (Daniel 7:13–14).

Another term applied to Jesus in the Gospels is 'Son of God'. Like the titles 'Messiah' and 'Son of Man', this expression is often used in the Hebrew Scriptures: the Jewish nation was often referred to as 'God's son', and the Kings of Israel, especially those who were descendants of David, were referred to in the same way. In the Gospels, however, this title was used to convey Jesus' close relationship with his heavenly Father. Hence, in this connection Matthew and Luke state with regard to Jesus: 'All things have been delivered to me by my Father; and no one knows the Son except the Father, and no one knows the Father except the Son and any one to whom the Son chooses to reveal him' (Matthew 11:27; Luke 10:22).

From the start of Jesus' ministry, his presence created divisions within the Jewish populace. John explains this by stating that when Jesus arrived, God's light came into the world. As a result, men and women were compelled to make decisions about the direction of their lives. They had to determine whether to be on God's side or against him (John 3: 16–21). In Matthew's Gospel Jesus explained what such a choice entails: 'No one can serve two masters; for either he will hate the one and love the other, or he will be devoted to the one and despise the other. You cannot serve God and mammon' (Matthew 6:24). Although the Gospels affirm that Jesus was loved by his followers, he was repeatedly opposed by religious authorities.

Because the Roman rulers of Palestine were deeply suspicious of anyone who fostered political unrest, it was not surprising that they too were disturbed by Jesus' activity. Yet the Gospels illustrate that Jesus was not a social agitator. Rather, he sought to criticize the religious leadership for their iniquity. The Pharisees and Sadducees were 'blind leaders of the blind' (Matthew 23:16–24); they had perverted the word of God. Although they appeared to be righteous, they were rotten. Thus he declared:

> 'Woe to you, scribes and Pharisees, hypocrites! for you are like whitewashed tombs, which outwardly appear beautiful, but within they are full of dead men's bones and all uncleanness. So you also outwardly appear righteous to men, but

within you are full of hypocrisy and iniquity. (Matthew 23:27)

Such criticism appears to have been a deliberate policy. Although Jesus is portrayed as spending short periods of time in remote areas teaching his disciples, the Gospels suggest that there was a particular moment when he decided the time had come to confront the leaders in Jerusalem. Various explanations have been given of this decisive step in Jesus' life. One view is that Jesus perceived that the time had come for his death; thus he set off for Jerusalem to fulfil God's providential scheme. In the Gospel of Luke, Jesus stated to his disciples: 'Behold, we are going up to Jerusalem, and everything that is written of the Son of Man by the prophets will be accomplished' (Luke 18:31). Another explanation is that Jesus made a deliberate gamble in going to Jerusalem which did not materialize: God did not save him from death; alternatively it has been suggested that Jesus went to Jerusalem because he had been to most parts of Palestine and he wished to continue his mission in the capital.

In any event, Jesus entered Jerusalem in such a way as to announce his Messiahship. He rode on an ass in accordance with the prophecy in Zechariah 9:9 ('Lo, your king comes to you; triumphant and victorious is he, humble and riding on an ass, on a colt the foal of an ass'). After this he went to the Temple where he drove out the moneychangers and those who sold pigeons (Mark 11:15–16). Subsequently Jesus gathered his disciples together for a final meal before his death. Together they followed the normal Jewish custom, giving thanks for the meal. Jesus then proceeded to break the bread on the table, and handed it to his disciples, proclaiming that it symbolized his body. He then handed them a cup of wine telling them that it was the blood of the covenant which is poured out for many. 'Truly, I say to you,' he declared, 'I shall not drink again of the fruit of the vine until the day when I drink it new in the kingdom of God' (Mark 14:22–25).

Eventually, Jesus was betrayed by one of his disciples,

arrested and tried. Here the Gospels provide various accounts of the events which took place. According to John's Gospel, the trial commenced in the house of Annas, the father-in-law of Caiaphas, the High Priest. However, because the Sanhedrin could not officially convene until daylight, its members did not gather together until the next morning. Initially Jesus refused to answer any questions about his teaching. Caiaphas then asked Jesus whether he was the Christ, the Son of the Blessed. In response, Jesus declared: 'I am', and added: 'and you will see the Son of man seated at the right hand of Power, and coming with the clouds of heaven' (Mark 14:61–62). This statement convinced the Sanhedrin of Jesus' guilt – it appears that it was not Jesus' claim that he was the Messiah that caused outrage, but his assertion that he would be coming on the clouds of heaven.

Jesus was then brought before Pilate. Here the charge of blasphemy was set aside: instead there was an attempt to persuade Pilate to confirm the Jewish sentence without stating any charge. However, when Pilate insisted on a charge, three accusations were made:

1. Jesus had perverted the Jewish nation.
2. Jesus had forbidden the payment of taxes.
3. Jesus had used the title 'king'.

Once Pilate interviewed Jesus, he realized that he had not actually violated any Roman law even though he had upset the Jewish community. In order to placate the Jewish officials, he permitted Jesus to be crucified, and a placard was nailed to his cross to indicate his offence: 'Jesus of Nazareth, King of the Jews'.

Death and Resurrection

All the writers of the Gospels agree that Jesus was raised on the third day after his crucifixion. Such a conviction was fundamental to the early Christians' understanding of the significance of Jesus' life. As Paul asserted: 'If Christ has not been raised, your faith is futile and you are still in your sins' (1 Corinthians 15:17). In the history of the

Church the earliest evidence for the resurrection event is found in the early sermons in Acts. Although this material was compiled at least thirty years after Jesus' death, it is based on earlier sources – this is illustrated by the fact that the language used in these early speeches is different from that used when the book was compiled in its final form.

Here the central message is the story of Jesus himself: Jesus had come to fulfil God's promises, and then died on the cross; subsequently he was raised to life. For these early Christians, Jesus fulfilled the prophecies in the Hebrew Scriptures: God was at work in his life, death and resurrection. He has now been exalted to Heaven, and the Holy Spirit has been given to the Church. Soon Jesus will return in glory, and those who hear this message should respond to the challenge of the Christian life. It appears from Acts that the qualification for an apostolic preacher was that he had seen the risen Christ – this was the condition made when the apostles came to appoint a successor to Judas Iscariot (Acts 1:21–22).

The second early evidence for Jesus' resurrection is Paul himself. Some time after Jesus' crucifixion, he had a vision of Jesus on the road to Damascus which served as a turning point in his life:

> For I would have you know, brethren, that the gospel which was preached by me is not man's gospel. For I did not receive it from man, nor was I taught it, but it came through a revelation of Jesus Christ. For you have heard of my former life in Judaism, how I persecuted the church of God violently and tried to destroy it; and I advanced in Judaism beyond many of my own age among my people, so extremely zealous was I for the traditions of my fathers. But when he who had set me apart before I was born, and had called me through his grace, was pleased to reveal his Son to me, in order that I might preach him among the Gentiles, I did not confer with flesh and blood, nor did I go up to Jerusalem to those who were apostles before me. (Galatians 1:11–17)

In another epistle Paul referred to the received tradition of Jesus' appearance to his disciples and to 500 followers:

> For I delivered to you as of first importance what I also
> received, that Christ died for our sins in accordance with the
> scriptures, that he was buried, that he was raised on the third
> day in accordance with the scriptures, and that he appeared
> to Cephas, then to the twelve. Then he appeared to more
> than five hundred brethren at one time. (1 Corinthians
> 15:3–6)

This is followed by an account of Jesus' appearance to
James and the apostles in which Paul included his own
experience of the risen Christ: 'Then he appeared to
James, then to all the apostles. Last of all, as to one
untimely born, he appeared also to me' (1 Corinthians
15:7–8).

Turning to the Gospels, the authors emphasize two
important features of the resurrection narrative: Jesus'
grave was empty, and he was seen by different individuals
at various times. Nonetheless, the Gospel accounts are not
easy to reconcile with one another. In Mark we are told
that some women who came to Jesus' grave on the Sunday
morning to finish the process of embalming his body
discovered that the stone slab used as door to the tomb
had been rolled back. When they entered the tomb, they
saw a young man sitting on the right side clothed in white.
When he saw that they were astonished by this sight, the
young man said: 'Do not be amazed; you seek Jesus of
Nazareth, who was crucified. He has risen, he is not here;
see the place where they laid him. But go, tell his disciples
and Peter that he is going before you to Galilee; there you
will see him, as he told you' (Mark 16:6–7). Terrified, the
women ran away and refrained from telling anyone what
they had seen. The following verses portray Jesus' appearance to Mary Magdalene, to two others as they were
walking in the country, and to eleven others – but this
passage is generally viewed as a later addition to the
Gospel.

In Luke's Gospel, as two disciples walk home to the
village of Emmaus they meet the risen Christ without
realizing who he is: 'While they were talking and discussing together, Jesus himself drew near and went with them.

But their eyes were kept from recognizing him' (Luke 24:15–16). Jesus asked them what they were discussing. In reply they explained about the empty tomb:

> Some women of our company amazed us. They were at the tomb early in the morning and did not find his body; and they came back saying that they had even seen a vision of angels, who said that he was alive. Some of those who were with us went to the tomb, and found it just as the women had said; but him they did not see. (Luke 24:22–24)

Eventually Jesus' identity was revealed as they were eating at table: 'And their eyes were opened and they recognized him; and he vanished out of their sight' (Luke 24:31). Later Jesus appeared to them again:

> Jesus himself stood among them. But they were startled and frightened, and supposed that they saw a spirit. And he said to them, 'Why are you troubled and why do questionings rise in your hearts? See my hands and my feet, that it is I myself; handle me, and see; for a spirit has not flesh and bones as you see that I have.' (Luke 24:36–39)

Mark's account is repeated in Matthew's Gospel with a number of additional details. After a great earthquake, an angel of the Lord appeared to them and urged them not to fear: 'Do not be afraid; for I know that you seek Jesus who was crucified. He is not here; for he has risen' (Matthew 28:5–6). He then instructed them to tell the disciples that Jesus had been raised and would appear in Galilee. They quickly departed and ran to tell the disciples, but were met by Jesus himself. They took hold of his feet and worshipped him; Jesus then urged them to tell the disciples to go to Galilee. When the eleven disciples encountered Jesus there, they worshipped him. When some expressed doubts about what they had experienced, Jesus said: 'All authority in heaven and on earth has been given to me. Go therefore and make disciples of all nations, baptizing them in the name of the Father and of the Son and of the Holy Spirit (Matthew 28:18–19).

In John's Gospel, Jesus appeared both in Jerusalem and

Galilee. Here only Mary Magdalene is mentioned as having discovered the empty tomb: 'Now on the first day of the week Mary Magdalene came to the tomb early, while it was still dark, and saw that the stone had been taken away from the tomb' (John 20:1). She then went to Peter and others to tell them what she had seen. They too then found the tomb empty with the grave clothes lying there. At this stage Mary saw two angels and Jesus himself though she did not initially recognize him. Jesus then said to her: 'Do not hold me, for I have not yet ascended to the Father; but go to my brethren and say to them, I am ascending to my Father and your Father, and to my God and your God' (John 20:17).

This event is followed by Jesus' appearances to his disciples in Jerusalem. On the evening of that day, Jesus came and stood among them and showed him his hands and his side. Thomas, however, was not with the other disciples when this occurred, and he declared: 'Unless I see in his hands the print of the nails, and place my finger in the mark of the nails, and place my hand in his side, I will not believe' (John 20:25). Eight days later Jesus came again and said to Thomas: 'Put your finger here, and see my hands; and put out your hand, and place it in my side; do not be faithless, but believing' (John 20:27). After this incident Jesus also appeared to the disciples by the Sea of Tiberias where he had breakfast with them.

Despite the varying Gospel accounts of Jesus' resurrection, this event was perceived by the early Church as the climax of his ministry. Through this supernatural event, Jesus' messianic role was confirmed. As Peter explained in Acts: 'Let all the house of Israel therefore know assuredly that God has made him both Lord and Christ, this Jesus whom you crucified' (Acts 2:36). For Paul, Jesus' death was an indispensable part of God's providential concern for humanity. Jesus, he believed, was still alive in the world, affecting the life of those who believed in him. 'It is no longer I who live, but Christ who lives in me', he declared (Galatians 2:20). Because of Jesus' resurrection, Paul asserted, he had found a new life. The resurrection of Jesus had one further crucial implication: just as Jesus died and was resurrected, so all of his followers will share in eternal life. According to Paul, Jesus is the first fruits of those who have fallen asleep (1 Corinthians 15:20). Thus, life beyond the grave is available to those who accept Jesus into their hearts.

The Kingdom of God

For the early Christians Jesus' coming signified the beginning of a new age. Assured that the promises of Scripture would be fulfilled, they believed that the Kingdom of God was at hand. Yet Jesus was anxious to point out that the Kingdom of God would have a different character from what was previously anticipated. Thus in Luke's Gospel, he announced to the Pharisees: 'The kingdom of God is not coming with signs to be observed; nor will they say, "Lo, here it is!" or "There!" for behold, the kingdom of God is in the midst of you' (Luke 17:20–21). On another occasion, he declared to his disciples: 'Truly, I say to you, whoever does not receive the kingdom of God like a child shall not enter it' (Mark 10:15). In both instances Jesus emphasized that the Kingdom of God will not involve political disruption, but rather a transformation of religious consciousness. God's new society is thus one in which his power is manifest in the life of those who believe in him.

Nonetheless, this new world order is not restricted to one's relationship with God; rather the Gospels stress that the Kingdom of God transcends the inward rule of God. In Luke's Gospel, Jesus stated: 'And men will come from east and west, and from north and south, and sit at table in the kingdom of God' (Luke 13:29). Again, at the Last Supper Jesus told his disciples: 'For I tell you that from now on I shall not drink of the fruit of the vine until the kingdom of God comes' (Luke 22:18). Matthew similarly recounts that Jesus declared that his followers will inherit the Kingdom which has been prepared from the foundation of the world (Matthew 25:34). Thus it appears that Jesus viewed the Kingdom of God as the Lord's rule over the lives of those who devote themselves to him as well as a new social and political transformation that will be demonstrated to all. These two aspects of the Kingdom are reflected in Paul's teaching. In Romans 14:17 he emphasized that the Kingdom of God is not food and drink but righteousness and peace and joy in the Holy Spirit, yet in 1 Corinthians he expected that the arrival of the Kingdom will effect a change in society: 'Then comes the end, when he delivers the kingdom to God the Father after destroying every rule and every authority' (1 Corinthians 15:24).

Throughout his ministry the Kingdom of God was the subject of much of Jesus' teaching. According to Jesus, entry into the new society offers the privilege of knowing God intimately as well as imposing responsibilities on the faithful. Hence at the beginning of Mark's Gospel, Jesus declared: 'The time is fulfilled, and the kingdom of God is at hand: repent, and believe in the gospel' (Mark 1:15). This theme is emphasized in the parable of the lost son who returns to his father (Luke 15:11-32). Here the theme of repentance is paramount as in the story of the Pharisee and the tax collector. Both went to pray in the Temple at the same time: the Pharisee was convinced of his righteousness, but the tax collector was overcome by a sense of sin and prayed: 'God, be merciful to me a sinner!' According to Jesus, it is was the tax collector, not the Pharisee, who had gained God's favour: 'I tell you, this man went down to his house justified rather than the other; for every one who exalts himself will be humbled, but he who humbles himself will be exalted' (Luke 18:14).

Repentance and forgiveness should be conceived as the preconditions of the Christian life, but such an attitude of mind must be supplemented by total devotion to God. For those who resolve to live in this way, there are important practical consequences. First, God's people must serve the Lord like the widow who put her last coin into the offering box in the Temple (Mark 12:41–44; Luke 21:1-4).

They should not behave ostentatiously; rather they ought to pray and fast in secret (Matthew 6:5–6). The faithful should make good use of God's provisions, always ready to face their master (Matthew 25:14–30). In sum, the central aim in life should be to learn more of God and his ways – it is worth sacrificing everything to participate in the reality of God's Kingdom.

Yet, it would be a mistake to think that Jesus' message was restricted to an individual's relationship with God. Much of his teaching concerns a person's responsibilities to others. This is most dramatically portrayed in the parable of the Good Samaritan. In answer to the question, 'Who is one's neighbour?', he stated:

> A man was going down from Jerusalem to Jericho, and he fell among robbers, who stripped him and beat him, and departed, leaving him half dead. Now by chance a priest was going down that road; and when he saw him he passed by on the other side. ... But a Samaritan, as he journeyed, came to where he was; and when he saw him, he had compassion, and went to him and bound up his wounds, pouring on oil and wine; then he set him on his own beast and brought him to an inn, and took care of him. And the next day he took out two denarii and gave them to the innkeeper, saying, 'Take care of him; and whatever more you spend, I will repay you when I come back.' (Luke 10:30–35)

For those who enter the Kingdom, not only will they share a new relationship with God, but their attitude to others will be transformed.

Jesus' parables also depict the coming of God's Kingdom in the future – this will be a time of reckoning. This is the point of Jesus' parable about the fishing net in Matthew's Gospel:

> The kingdom of heaven is like a net which was thrown into the sea and gathered fish of every kind; when it was full, men drew it ashore and sat down and sorted the good into vessels but threw away the bad. So it will be at the close of the age. The angels will come out and separate the evil from the righteous. (Matthew 13:47–49)

Elsewhere Jesus stated that the climax of the Kingdom will be a feast, yet not everyone will gain admission (Mattthew 22:1–14; Luke 14:15–24). Matthew's Gospel emphasizes that no one can know when this great event will take place: 'Of that day and hour no one knows, not even the angels of heaven, nor the Son, but the Father only' (Matthew 24:36). Thus one must be in a state of readiness like the bridesmaids at a wedding (Matthew 25:1–13).

As a sign of the Kingdom, the Gospels record Jesus' miraculous acts; such events indicate that God's Kingdom had arrived. Thus when John the Baptist sent some of his followers to ask Jesus whether he was the Messiah, Jesus declared: 'Go and tell John what you hear and see: the blind receive their sight and the lame walk, lepers are cleansed and the deaf hear, and the dead are raised up, and the poor have good news preached to them' (Matthew 11:4–5). This proclamation was based on a passage in Isaiah (Isaiah 35:5–6) which was generally believed to refer to a future messianic age. In John's Gospel, Jesus' miracles are called 'signs'; by means of these actions, men and women perceive that a new society has been inaugurated by Jesus. Hence, in John 2:11, Jesus is described as revealing his glory by changing water into wine. Later, the raising of Lazarus is described as the means by which the Son of God will be glorified (John 11:4).

The miracles, however, do not simply announce the arrival of God's Kingdom; they also highlight various aspects of Jesus' teaching. First, they stress that by following Jesus individuals can be freed from the mastery of sin. This was so particularly for those at the margin of society – it was just such individuals to whom Jesus' words were specifically addressed. Second, just as the healing miracles illustrate Jesus' capacity to release individuals from the power of sin, so other miracles dealing with nature display Jesus' rule over all of creation. Third, Jesus' miraculous feeding of thousands highlight his messianic role: it is he who will feed God's people. Finally, Jesus' resurrection of those who have died exhibits that the promise of eternal life will be fufilled.

The Jewish View of Jesus

From New Testament times Jesus has been understood by Christians as the risen Christ who sits at the right hand of the Father. As God's Anointed he ushered in the Kingdom of God in which the Old Torah is superseded; through his life and death, forgiveness, atonement and salvation are offered to all. Jesus summons every person to enter into a new covenant with God based on divine love and grace. In the light of this conception of Christ, the doctrines of the Incarnation and the Trinity became central tenets of the faith: for the faithful Jesus is seen as the Second Person of the Trinity who at the Second Coming will return to judge the living and the dead and terminate human history.

According to the New Testament, Jesus attracted a large circle of followers during his lifetime. However, from the first century CE to the present the Jewish community has rejected his claims to Messiahship. For most Jews the central difference between Judaism and Christianity concerns the doctrine of God. For over two thousand years, Jews have daily recited the *Shema*: 'Hear O Israel: The Lord our God is one Lord' (Deuteronomy 6:4). Given this idea of God, it is not surprising that in the early rabbinic period Christianity was attacked for its doctrine of the Incarnation. According to rabbinic sources, the belief that God was in Christ is heretical; the doctrine that God is both Father and Son was viewed as a dualistic theology.

As time passed the doctrine of the Trinity was bitterly denounced as well. Christian exegetes in the Middle Ages for example interpreted the *Shema*, with its three references to God, as referring to the Trinity. Jewish commentators maintained that in this prayer there is a reference only to one God and not three persons in the Godhead. Christians often asserted that Jewish polemics against the Trinity were based on an inadequate understanding. Although some of these criticisms were uninformed, all Jewish thinkers rejected trinitarianism as incompatible with monotheism. Modern Jewish thought is equally critical of any attempt to harmonize the belief in God's unity with the concept of a triune God. Contemporary Jewish theologians of all degrees of observance affirm that Judaism is fundamentally incompatible with what they perceive as the polytheistic character of trinitarian belief.

Connected with the Jewish rejection of the doctrines of the Incarnation and the Trinity, Jews have consistently denied the Christian claim that Jesus is the Messiah for a number of reasons. First, according to Judaism it is obvious that Jesus did not fulfil the messianic expectations as recorded in Scripture, post-biblical literature, and as elaborated by the rabbis. He did not restore the kingdom of David to its former glory; nor did he gather in the dispersed ones of Israel and restore all the laws of the Torah that were in abeyance (such as the sacrificial cult). He did not compel Israel to walk in the way of the Torah, nor did he rebuild the Temple and usher in a new order in the world and nature. In other words, Jesus did not inaugurate a cataclysmic change in history. Universal peace, in which there is neither war nor competition, did not come about on earth. Thus for Jews, Jesus did not fulfil the prophetic messianic hope in a redeemer who would bring political and spiritual redemption as well as earthly blessings and moral perfection to the human race.

A second objection to Jesus concerns the Christian claim that he possesses a special relationship with God. This notion was repeatedly stated in the Gospels. In Matthew, for example, we read: 'No one knows the Son except the Father; and no one knows the Father, except the Son' (Matthew 11:27). In John's Gospel Jesus declared: 'I am the way, and the truth, and the life; no one comes to the Father but by me. If you had known me, you would have known my Father also; henceforth you know him and have seen him' (John 14:6–7). This concept undermines the Jewish conviction that God is equally near to all.

The third objection to Jesus arises from his attitude

toward sin and sinners. The traditional task of the prophets was to castigate Israel for rejecting God's law, not to
forgive sin. Jesus, however, took upon himself the power
to do this. Thus he declared with regard to a paralytic:
' "For which is easier, to say, 'Your sins are forgiven', or to
say, 'Rise and walk'? But that you may know that the Son
of man has authority on earth to forgive sins" – he then
said to the paralytic – "Rise, take up your bed and go
home" ' (Matthew 9:5–6). When Jesus said to a woman of
ill-repute, 'Your sins are forgiven' his companions were
shocked. 'Who is this, who even forgives sins?' they asked
(Luke 7:48–49). It is not surprising that this was their
reaction since such a usurpation of God's prerogative was
without precedent. A similar objection applies to the
Gospel record that Jesus performed miracles on his own
authority without making reference to God (John
5:18–21).

A fourth objection to Jesus concerns his otherworldli-
ness. The rabbis sought to provide adequate social legisla-
tion, but Jesus had a view different from theirs. To him
poverty was not a deprivation; on the contrary, he regarded it as meritorious. For example, Jesus told a potential
disciple: 'If you would be perfect, go, sell what you possess
and give to the poor, and you will have treasure in heaven;
and come, follow me' (Matthew 19:21). In the Sermon on
the Mount, Jesus proclaimed: 'Blessed are you poor, for
yours is the kingdom of God' (Luke 6:20). In Jewish eyes,
however, poverty is an evil; the sages sought to alleviate it
by enacting laws to tax the wealthy for the benefit of the
poor.

A further objection to Jesus concerns his admonition to
break all human ties: 'Whoever of you does not renounce
all that he has cannot be my disciple' (Luke 14:33). Or
again, 'Who is my mother, and who are my brothers? ...
Here are my mother and my brothers! For whoever does
the will of my Father in heaven is my brother, and sister,
and mother' (Matthew 12:48–50). Similarly, he declared:
'Call no man your father on earth, for you have one
Father, who is in heaven' (Matthew 23:9). In contrast to

these views, Judaism asserts that persons can not live a full life unless they are members of a family and are well integrated into the larger community. The renunciation of family bonds is regarded as a travesty of the created order.

Finally, Jesus' teaching is rejected by Jews because his interpretation of Jewish law is at variance with rabbinic tradition. Though at one point in the Gospels Jesus declared that no change should be made in the law (Matthew 5:17), he disregarded a number of important precepts. Several times on the Sabbath, for example, Jesus cured individuals who were not dangerously ill, in violation of the rabbinic precept that the Sabbath law can only be broken for the saving and preserving of life (Matthew 12:9–14; Luke 13:10–16; 14:3–6). Conversely, Jesus was more strict about the law of divorce that the Pharisees. Thus he stated:

> It was also said, 'Whoever divorces his wife, let him give her a certificate of divorce.' But I say to you that every one who divorces his wife, except on the ground of unchastity, makes her an adultress; and whoever marries a divorced woman commits adultery. (Matthew 5:31–32)

Another serious divergence from traditional Jewish law was Jesus' view that the ritual washing of hands before meals was unimportant. In response to the Pharisees' criticism of his disciples for eating without first washing their hands, he rebuked the Pharisees for not keeping the ethical commandments; 'These are,' he stated, 'what defile a man: but to eat with unwashed hands does not defile a man' (Matthew 15:20).

Jesus also violated the laws regarding fasts. The Gospels record that when the Pharisees were fasting, Jesus' disciples did not fast. When questioned about this, he replied: 'Can the wedding guests mourn as long as the bridegroom is with them? The days will come, when the bridegroom is taken away from them, and then they will fast' (Matthew 9:15). When the Pharisees criticized the disciples for plucking wheat on the Sabbath, Jesus proclaimed: 'The Son of man is lord of the sabbath' (Matthew 12:8).

The vision of messianic redemption brought about by Jesus is therefore at odds with traditional Judaism. To the Jewish mind, God's covenant with the Jews is intact. The Messiah has not yet come, and as has been the case throughout Jewish history the Jews are still obligated to keep God's commandments: their task is to become God's co-partners in maintaining and preserving righteousness, justice, and peace in an as yet unredeemed world. For the Jewish populace of the first century Jesus was regarded simply as one preacher among many, a false Messiah who had failed to fulfil the scriptural predictions of redemption and deliverance.

5

Early Rabbinic Expectations

The destruction of Jerusalem and the Temple in 70 CE profoundly affected Jewish life and led to intensified longing for messianic deliverance. With the loss of both the Northern and Southern Kingdoms Jews looked to the advent of the messianic age when the nation would be restored to its ancient homeland. As we have seen, in this milieu a Jewish sect emerged during this period which believed that Jesus would return again to bring about the fulfilment of biblical prophecy. Although mainstream Jewry rejected Jesus as the long-awaited Messiah, the Jewish community continued to long for divine deliverance, and in 132 a messianic revolt against Rome was led by the warrior Simeon bar Kochba. This rebellion was inspired by the conviction that God sought to overthrow Roman oppression. When this uprising was crushed, Jews put forward the year of messianic deliverance until the fifth century. In fulfilment of this prediction, a figure named Moses appeared in Crete, declaring that he would be able to lead Jews across the seas to Judaea. However, after this plan failed, Jews continued to engage in messianic speculation, believing that they could determine the date of their deliverance on the basis of scriptural texts – their reflections are recorded in a number of midrashic sources. In the ninth century the rabbinic scholar and philosopher Saadiah Gaon continued this tradition of messianic calculation. During these centuries of heightened messianic awareness, a series of pseudo-Messiahs such as Abu Isa al-Ispahani, Serene and Yudghan appeared, and the traveller Eldad Ha-Dani brought reports of the ten lost tribes, an event which stimulated the Jewish desire to return to Zion. Later during the period of the Crusades, messianic expectation intensified as Jews faced persecution and death – in this milieu these tragedies signified the birth pangs of the Messiah.

The Mishnaic and Talmudic Periods

Despite the overwhelming victory of the Romans in the first century, Jewish revolts against Rome continued into the next century. When the emperor Trajan invaded the East up to the Persian coast, a number of uprisings took place among Babylonian Jews. Further, similar riots occurred in many parts of the Roman diaspora. As the fourth-century Christian scholar Eusebius observed, the Jewish community was massacred in these rebellions:

> In Alexandria and the rest of the East, and in Cyrene as well ... (the Jews) rushed into a faction fight against their Greek fellow citizens ... against them the emperor sent Marcius Turbo with land and sea forces, including a contingent of cavalry. He pursued the war against them relentlessly in a long series of battles, destroying many thousands of Jews. (Eusebius, 1965, 154–5)

Between 114 and 117 Jewish centres in Alexandria, Cyrenaica, Egypt and Cyprus were devastated. However, after Trajan's death, his successor Hadrian abandoned the quest to extend the empire eastwards, leaving the Jewish diaspora in Babylonia free from Roman domination.

During this period of unrest messianic speculation became a central feature of Jewish life – the rabbis of the latter half of the first and the early half of the second century were convinced that the Jewish people would be liberated from the yoke of Roman oppression and that the nation would be restored to political independence. Therefore the scholars of the time immediately after the destruction of the Second Temple engaged in debate regarding the date of the Messiah's coming. Rabbi Joshua, for example, stated: 'In *Nisan* (the 14th day) were they (the children of Israel) redeemed, in *Nisan* will they again be redeemed.' This opinion was based on Exodus 12:42: 'It was a night of watching by the Lord, to bring them out of the land of Egypt; so this same night is a night of watching kept to the Lord by all the people of Israel throughout their generations.' Rabbi Eliezer, on the other hand, maintained that divine redemption would occur in *Tishri* on New Year's Day on the basis of Psalm 81:4–5 ('For it is a statute for Israel, an ordinance of the God of Jacob. He made it a decree in Joseph, when he went out over the land of Egypt'), and Isaiah 27:13 ('And in that day a great trumpet will be blown, and those who were lost in the land of Assyria and those who were driven out to the land of Egypt will come and worship the Lord on the holy mountain at Jerusalem') (*Rosh Hashanah* 11b).

Other scholars were preoccupied with the birth pangs of the Messiah. Thus Rabbi Eliezer ben Hyrcanus argued that this epoch would last forty years. According to the Talmud such a conviction was based on Psalm 95:10, 'For forty years I loathed that generation'. According to another passage, it was based on a combination of Deuteronomy 8:3 ('And he humbled you and let you hunger and fed you with manna' forty years in the wilderness), and Psalm 90:15 ('Make us glad as many days as thou hast afflicted us, and as many years as we have seen evil') (*Sanhedrin* 99a). Other scholars held different views about the length of this period: Rabbi Jose the Galilean, sixty years, and Rabbi Eleazar ben Azariah, seventy years. Yet despite such disagreement, Jews who lived during the first century and the early part of the second century believed they were living at the close of the fifth millennium – this, they were convinced, was the last epoch before the thousand years of peace which would be inaugurated by the Messiah.

In such a milieu a revolt was led in 132 by Simeon bar Kochba (also called bar Kosiba) who was viewed by many as the long-awaited Messiah who would deliver his people – this uprising was supported by Rabbi Akiva and other scholars from Jamnia in the wake of Hadrian's programme of Hellenization. This revolt was inspired by the

conviction that God would liberate the Jews from their
oppressors – they would regain control of their country
and rebuild the Temple. Although the rebels fought
valiantly, the Romans crushed the uprising. Hundreds of
thousands of Jews were slaughtered, and Judaea was
devastated. In 135 the rebellion came to an end with the
fall of Bethar, south-west of Jerusalem. According to
tradition, this event took place on the 9th of *Av*, the same
day as the destruction of the First and Second Temples.
During the course of the campaign bar Kochba was killed,
and Rabbi Akiva was flayed alive.

Following the collapse of this rebellion, the date of the
coming of the Messiah was pushed forward – it was
estimated that it would occur 400 years after the destruction of Judah. This figure was naturally assumed because it
corresponds to the period of Egyptian exile as recorded in
Scripture. Hence Rabbi Dosa maintained that the Messiah
will come in the fifth century – this calculation was based
on a comparison between Psalm 90:15 (quoted earlier)
and Genesis 15:13 ('Then the Lord said to Abraham,
"Know of a surety that your descendants will be sojour-
ners in a land that is not theirs, and will be slaves there,
and they will be oppressed for four hundred years"')
(*Sanhedrin* 99a). A similar view was expressed by Judah ha-
Nasi who maintained that the coming of the Messiah will
take place 365 years after the destruction of Jerusalem;
this number corresponds to the days of the solar year and
is based on Isaiah 63:4 ('For the day of vengeance was in
my heart and my year of redemption has come') (that is,
one year for every day in the solar year) (*Sanhedrin* 99a).
Similarly, Rabbi Hanina believed that the Messiah would
come 400 years after the fall of Jerusalem. 'If 400 years
after the destruction a man says to you "Buy my field,
which is worth one thousand dinars, for one dinar", do
not buy it', he declared.

In connection with this messianic date, there is a legend
about a mysterious scroll discovered in the archives of
Rome. Regarding this discovery, Rabbi Hanan ben
Tahilpa sent word to Rabbi Joseph:

I happened upon a man who had in his possession a scroll written both in Assyrian and Hebrew script. I asked him where he got it, and he told me that he had hired himself out as a servant in the Roman army, and that he had found this scroll in the archives of Rome. In it is written: 4291 years after creation the present order of the world will come to an end. The Wars of the Serpents will then take place, and the Wars of Gog and Magog, following which the messianic age will set in. (*Sanhedrin* 97b)

A similar calculation was allegedly revealed to Rabbi Judah by the prophet Elijah: 'The world will endure no less than 85 jubilees (4250 years), and in the last jubilee the son of David will come' (*Sanhedrin* 97b).

As the fifth century approached, messianic expectations were heightened. With the collapse of the Roman empire, the Jewish nation believed it was living in the final days before the advent of the messianic age. In this milieu a pseudo-Messiah appeared in about 448 among the Jews in Crete, and proclaimed his messianic mission to the Jewish inhabitants of the island. Business was neglected and daily pursuits abandoned as Jews gathered together to follow him. As a new Moses, he declared that he would lead them through the sea to the Promised Land just as Moses had done in ancient times. Persuaded of his Messiahship, men, women and children followed him to the sea. Standing on a promontory projecting into the water, Moses told them to jump into the ocean. As a consequence a number drowned, whereas others were rescued by sailors and subsequently embraced the Christian faith. This tragedy, as well as the failure of the Messiah to appear as predicted, led to a lessening of messianic expectations. Yet the hope of redemption continued to remain a major feature of rabbinic speculation in the centuries which followed.

Rabbinic Apocalypses

During the sixth and seventh centuries Jewish scholars continued to engage in messianic calculation and composed a number of speculative works such as *The Signs of the Messiah* and *Agada of the Messiah*. In all likelihood these writings were produced because of the crises in Babylon during the reign of Kavadh which led to the revolt of the exilarch Mar Zuta II at the beginning of the sixth century. Alternatively, they may have emerged when the Persians conquered Syria and Palestine in the next century. In any event the return of the Byzantines under Heraclius in 629 led to the persecution of Jews which continued until the rise of Islam. The victories of the Arabs and the collapse of the Persian and Byzantine empires fuelled the flames of messianic speculation – as the followers of Muhammad embarked on their campaigns, the Jewish community expressed its hopes for redemption in various compositions.

The first among these works was *Pirke de Rabbi Eliezer*, a text of Palestinian origin which was edited in the eighth century. In chapter 28 the author explains that in Abraham's vision of the 'covenant between the pieces' in Genesis 15, God had revealed the events which would befall his descendants. On the basis of Genesis 15:9 ('Bring me a heifer three years old, a she-goat three years old, a ram three years old, a turtledove, and a young pigeon'), four empires would reign over the Jewish nation: the heifer was identified with Rome; the she-goat with Greece; the ram with Persia, the ox with Ishmael (the Arabs); and the pigeon with Israel. Another view is that five empires would rule over the Jewish people, based on Genesis 15:12 ('As the sun was going down, a deep sleep fell upon Abram, and lo, a dread (Rome), and great (Persia) darkness (Greece) fell (Babylon) upon him (Ishmael)' – in this verse various words were identified with different empires. The implication is that Messiah will come after the emergence of Islam.

The text also specifies the date of messianic deliverance. Thus Rabbi Joshua stated:

> Abraham took his sword and divided them, each one into two parts, as it is said, 'And he took him all these and he divided them in the midst' (Genesis 15:10). Were it not for the fact that he divided them, the world would not have been able to

exist, but because he divided them he weakened their strength, and he brought each part against its corresponding part, as it is said, 'And he laid each half over against the other.' (Here Joshua is referring to the division of the Roman empire which occurred after the death of Theodosius in 395; thus the Western empire came to an end in 476.) And the young pigeon, he left alive, as it is said, 'But the bird he divided not', hence thou mayest learn that there was not any other bird there except a young pigeon (Israel). The bird of prey came down upon them to scatter them and to destroy them. The bird of prey is naught else but David, the son of Jesse, who is compared to a speckled bird of prey, as it is said, 'Is mine heritage unto me as a speckled bird of prey?' (Jeremiah 12:9). When the sun was about to rise in the east, Abraham sat down and waved his scarf over them, so that the bird of prey could not prevail over them until the raven came. (in Silver, 1978, 38–9)

In this text the writer explains that the Messiah did not emerge in the fifth century as predicted; rather, he will come after the conquests of the Arabs (*Midrash Rabba Ber.* 50:5).

Commenting on this passage, Rabbi Eleazar ben Azariah stated that 'from this incident thou mayest learn that the rule of the four kingdoms (Persia, Greece, Rome and Arab) will last only one day according to the day of the Holy One, blessed be he' (one day = 1000 years). Assuming that the building of the Temple took place in 352, the end of the last kingdom would be c. 648. Rabbi Eleazar ben Arak, however, offered a different interpretation:

Verily, it is so according to thy word, as it is said, 'He hath made me desolate and faint all the day', except for two thirds of an hour (of God). Know that it is so. Come and see, for when the sun turns to set in the west, during two thirds of an hour its power is weakened, and it has no light; likewise, whilst the evening is not yet come, the light of Israel shall arise, as it is said, 'And it shall come to pass that at evening time there shall be light' (Zechariah 14:7). (in Silver, 1978, 40)

Since two thirds of God's hour would be about 28 years,

the deliverance of Israel would occur in 620 (rather than 648).

An alternative prediction was advanced in chapter 30 of this work by Rabbi Ishmael:

> In the future the children of Ishmael will do fifteen things in the land (of Israel), in the latter days, and they are ... and they will build a building in the Holy Place; and two brothers will arise over them, princes at the end; and in their days the branch of the son of David will arise, as it is said, 'And in the days of those kings shall the God of heaven set up a kingdom which will never be destroyed.' (in Silver, 1978, 40)

In this passage the building referred to is the Mosque of Omar; in all likelihood the brothers are Moawiya, who was appointed governor of Syria and Palestine in 639 and in 661 was proclaimed calif in Jerusalem, and Ziyad who became ruler of Basra and the eastern provinces in 665. Hence the author would have expected the advent of the Messiah in the latter half of the seventh century.

Another composition dating from this period, the *Book of Elijah*, contains a similar prediction about the Messianic Age. Here the angel Michael showed Elijah the regions of Heaven and revealed the end of human history. The Messiah, he explained, will come during the reign of the last king of Persia. The rabbis then debated his identity: one referred to him as Armilius, another Cyrus. Simeon ben Yohai, however, stated that his name is Kersra (Chosroes II who conquered Jerusalem in 614). Another apocalypse, *The Chapters of the Messiah*, indicates that the conquest of the Arabs will be followed by messianic deliverance.

In the next century, the *Revelations of Simeon ben Yohai* expresses the view that the Muslims are God's instrument in bringing about the conquest of Rome, and places the advent of the Messianic Age immediately after the collapse of the Omayyad dynasty. In this work Rabbi Simeon ben Yohai is portrayed in his cave contemplating Numbers 24:21: 'And he looked on the Kenite.' Complaining to God, he cried: 'Is it not enough what the kingdom of

Edom has done unto us? Must thou now send upon us the kingdom of Ishmael?' In response, the angel Metatron declared: 'Fear not, man, the Lord, blessed be he, brings this kingdom of Ishmael upon you only to deliver you from this wicked one.' When Rabbi Simeon demanded proof for this claim, the angel appealed to the Bible: 'Go, set a watchman, let him announce what he sees. When he sees riders, horsemen in pairs, riders on asses, riders on camels, let him listen diligently, very diligently' (Isaiah 21:6–7). Here the riders on camels (Arabs) precede the rider on the ass (the Messiah); the angel then outlines the history of Islam from Muhammad through the Omayyad califs.

After the death of Merwan II, the angel stated that a cruel king will rule for three months; then the wicked king (Byzantium) will appear, return the Jewish nation to Jerusalem and rebuild the Temple. However, the cruel king Armilius will emerge, wage war against the Messiah, and drive Israel into the wilderness for forty-five days where the Messiah will die. Then the Messiah ben David will arrive. Although the Jewish people will initially reject him, they will ultimately accept him as Messiah. He will then slay Armilius and gather together all Israel in Jerusalem which will be cleansed of all sinners as well as the uncircumcised. Heavenly Jerusalem will then descend and Israel will dwell in peace for two thousand years; this era will be followed by a final judgment.

A further source dating from this period is the *Midrash of the Ten Kings* which lists the kings who will rule over the world before the advent of the messianic age: (1) God; (2) Nimrod; (3) Joseph; (4) Solomon; (5) Ahab; (6) Nebuchadnezzar; (7) Cyrus; and (8) Alexander. The *midrash* then relates the destruction of the Temple and establishment of the academy at Jamnia, the rebellion of Bar Kochba and the Hadrianic persecutions. Then follows prophecies disclosed to Rabbi Simeon ben Yohai. Here it is predicted that the Messiah will come during the reign of the two brothers (in the latter half of the seventh century). Yet, if the Jewish people are not worthy of his deliverance, then his arrival will be postponed until the collapse of the Omayyad dynasty. Near the end of this work, it is claimed that the ninth king will be the Messiah ben David and that the tenth will be God himself.

Another work, *The Prayer of Rabbi Simeon ben Yohai*, is based on the *Revelations of Simeon ben Yohai*. However, whereas the *Revelations* implies that after the death of Merwan II (750) the Messiah will come, this text continues the history to the time of the Crusades. A similar date of the advent of the Messiah is implied by the *Alphabet of Rabbi Akiva*, a treatise on the mystical significance of the Hebrew alphabet:

> Eight hundred years after the destruction of the Second Temple the Kedarenes will decrease in number ... at the end of 295 years, according to the calendar of the gentiles (dating from the Hegira AD 622), this kingdom will vanish from the earth ... at the end of 304 years according to their calendar the Son of David will come, God willing. (in Silver, 1978, 48)

Thus the Messiah was expected in the tenth century. In another apocalyptic work, *The Story of Daniel*, the messianic age is also predicted at this time. Finally, *The Book of Zerubbabel* states that the Messiah will come 990 years after the destruction of the Temple (1060).

Pre-Crusade Messianic Speculation

In addition to midrashic literature, the tenth-century scholar and philosopher Saadia Gaon engaged in messianic speculation. In the eighth chapter of his *Emunot ve-Deot*, his commentary on the Book of Daniel, and his *Sefer ha-Galui* he examined the nature of messianic prediction and the final redemption. In *Emunot ve-Deot* he sought to explain the meaning of various figures given to Daniel. Thus concerning Daniel 12:6–7 ('"How long shall it be till the end of these wonders?" The man clothed in linen, who was above the waters of the stream, raised his right hand and his left hand toward heaven; and I heard him swear by him who lives for ever that it would be for a time, two times, and half a time'), Saadia maintained that here the expression 'time and a half' refers to 1335 years (the days are in this instance to be reckoned as years). The term 'times' refers to the two periods when the kingdom of Israel was in existence. The first period consisted of 480 years up to the creation of the First Temple; the second period lasted 410 years until its destruction. This totals 890 years, half of which is 445 years. Therefore 'time and a half' = 1335 years.

The second figure is given in Daniel 12:11: 'And from the time that the continual burnt offering is taken away, and the abomination that makes desolate is set up, there shall be a thousand two hundred and ninety days.' In Saadia's view, this expression refers to an event which took place during the period of the Second Temple, 45 years after the first prophecy of Daniel, thereby producing the number 1335. A further prophecy is found in Daniel 8:14: 'And he said to him, "For two thousand and three hundred evenings and mornings; then the sanctuary shall be restored to its rightful state."' This number – 2300 – is to be divided by two since both nights and days are included, producing 1150. This date refers to an event which occurred 185 years after the first prophecy to Daniel, again producing the number 1335. Arguably Saadia believed the period began in the third year of the reign of King Cyrus when the Jewish people were allowed to return to Judah from Babylonia – this would have been 367 BCE. Following this calculation, the Messiah will arrive in 978 CE. A Karaite contemporary of Saadia, Salmon ben Yeroham, arrived at the same conclusion in his commentary on the Book of Daniel; in the next century the Karaite scholar and commentator Japheth Ha-Levi stated that it was common among the rabbis to count the 1335 day-years from the third year of the reign of King Cyrus.

As the year 978 approached, expectations mounted throughout the Jewish world. In the Rhineland, the Jewish community sent an inquiry to the School of Jerusalem in 960 requesting verification of the report of the coming of the Messiah. The reply expressed dismay: 'As regards your question about the coming of the Messiah, you do not even deserve a reply. For you do not believe in the words of our sages and their signs (which they specified for the identification of the true Messiah), and these have not as yet come to pass.' Further evidence that Jews in Germany were enthusiastically anticipating the coming of the Messiah at this time is implied in Benjamin of Tudela's *Itinerary*, which contains an insertion from an earlier account:

> If we were not afraid that the appointed time has not yet been reached, we should have gathered together, but we dare not do so until the time for song has arrived, when the messengers will come and say continually: 'The Lord be exalted'. Meanwhile they send missives to one another, saying: 'Be ye strong in the law of Moses, and do ye, mourners for Zion, and ye, mourners for Jerusalem, entreat the Lord, and may the supplications of those that wear the garments of mourning be received through their merits.' (in Silver, 1978, 53)

At the same time Hasdai Ibn Shaprut inquired of Joseph, King of the Khazars, when messianic deliverance would take place:

> Again I would ask of my master the King, to let me know whether there is among you any tradition concerning the time of the end, for which we have been waiting these many years, during which time we have been going from one captivity to another, and from one exile to another. For one must be very strong, indeed, to refrain from inquiring about it. How can I be silent about the destruction of the Temple in our glory, and about the remnant escaped from the sword, which has passed through fire and water? We who were many are now few, and are fallen from our high estate and dwell in exile. We have no retort to those who say to us daily, 'Every people has a kingdom, but you have none.' (in Silver, 1978, 53)

In response the king declared:

> You ask furthermore concerning the end of wonders. Our eyes are turned to the Lord our God, and to the wise men of Israel in the academies of Jerusalem and Babylon, for we are very far from Zion, but we have heard that because of the sins

of the people, the calculations have gone astray and we know nothing ... We have nothing but the prophecy of Daniel. May the God of Israel hasten the redemption and gather our exiled and scattered people in our lifetime and in yours, and in the lifetime of the house of Israel, who love his name. (in Silver, 1978, 53–4)

Among the Karaites of this period Japheth Ha-Levi noted that it was commonly believed that the advent of the Messiah would take place after 2300 years, beginning with the Exodus; according to Karaite chronology, this occurred in 1332 BCE – hence the Messiah was foreseen as coming in 968 CE. Believing himself to be living in this messianic milieu, the Karaite scholar Sahl ben Mazliah Ha-Kohen stated in the *Sefer Tokahot*: 'And behold the days of the visitation of the nations are at hand, and the time of the salvation of Israel is also at hand. May God hasten that day and deliver us from the two women (the rabbinic academies of Sura and Pumbeditha) and cause the Messiah ben David to rule over us.' With pride he pointed to the Karaite communities which had been established in Jerusalem which were continually praying for the coming of the messianic age.

During this period several messianic figures appeared. The first was Abu Isa al-Ispahani. According to the Karaite scholar al-Kirkisani, he lived during the reign of Caliph Abd al-Malik ibn Marwan who ruled from 685 to 705; the Arabic historian al-Shahrastani placed him during the reigns of the Omayyad caliphs Marwan ibn Muhammad (744–50) and al Mansur (745–75). In any event Abu Isa stated that he was a prophet and herald of the Messiah. When he revolted against the Muslims, he was joined by many Persian Jews. After several years, this rebellion was suppressed: his army was defeated near the ancient city of Rhagae and Abu Isa was killed. His followers, however, did not believe he had died; instead they maintained he disappeared into a cave. Another tradition states that he placed his followers in a circle which he drew with a myrtle branch enabling them to remain beyond the reach of the enemy. Only Abu Isa rode out of this circle to attack the Muslims. Subsequently he went beyond the desert to prophesy among the 'Sons of Moses'.

The sect founded by Abu Isa was known as the Isunians (or Isfahanians) who continued to exist until the time of al-Kirkisani in the tenth century. According to tradition, Abu Isa was an illiterate tailor who wrote his books through prophetic inspiration. In his view five prophets preceded the advent of the Messiah. On the basis of Psalm 119:164 ('Seven times a day I praise thee'), Abu Isa believed himself to be the last harbinger of messianic redemption and ordained seven daily prayers for his disciples even though he did not reject the recitation of the *Shema* and the *Amidah* or the observance of the holy days as practised by the rabbis. Nonetheless in his revolt against various rabbinic doctrines and practices, he was a forerunner of the Karaites. As for Abu Isa's view of other faiths, tradition relates that he was tolerant of both Christianity and Islam. As al-Kirkisani related, he

> acknowledged the prophecy of Jesus, the son of Mary, and the prophecy of the master of the Mohammedans, contending that each of these two was sent to his own people. He advocated the study of the Gospels and of the Koran, as well as the knowledge of their interpretation, and he maintained that the Mohammedans and Christians were both guided in their faith by what they possessed, just as the Jews were guided in their faith by what they possessed. (in Silver, 1978, 55–6)

Another pseudo-Messiah of this period was Serene from Shirin who declared he was the Messiah in about 720 and promised to liberate Jerusalem from the Arabs. According to Isador Pacensis writing in 750, he attracted a large number of followers among Spanish and French Jews who abandoned their homes and possessions and set out to meet him. In accordance with his self-designated role as the Messiah, Serene rejected various talmudic laws, including those dealing with forms of prayer, forbidden foods, marriage contracts, and marriages between close relations. Eventually he was captured and taken to the calif, Yazid II. In response to cross-examination, he denied that he had been serious about his messianic claims – his aim was to mislead and mock his followers. The calif then handed Serene over to the Jewish community; according to the responsum of Natronai Gaon, Serene and his followers were declared guilty of violating rabbinic law.

Another eighth-century messianic figure was Yudghan of Hamadan (also known as al-Rai) who was a follower of Abu Isa. He claimed to be a prophet of his disciples (the Yudghanites) who viewed him as the Messiah. According to al-Kirkisani in his book *Gardens and Parks*, the Yudghan-ites 'prohibit meat and intoxicating drinks, observe many prayers and fasts, and assert that the Sabbath and holidays are at present no longer obligatory'. The Muslim historian al-Shahrastani further stated in his book *Religions and Sects* that Yudghan believed the Torah contains an allegorical and literal interpretation different from that held by rabbinic scholars. Again, the Karaite exegete Japheth ben Ali stated that the Yudghanites view the holidays as symbols and maintain that after the destruction of the Temple, many laws are no longer in force.

In the second half of the ninth century, the traveller Eldad Ha-Dani brought reports of the ten lost tribes whose restoration formed part of the scheme of messianic redemption. Although he did not view himself as the Messiah, his accounts heightened messianic aspirations. Professing himself to belong to the tribe of Dan, he argued that the tribes of Dan, Naphtali, Gad and Asher formed an independent kingdom in Havilah, the land of gold (near Ethiopia), under their king Addiel. These tribes, he maintained, were constantly at war with their neighbours. Eldad also referred to the 'Sons of Moses' who lived nearby but were cut off from the world by an impassable river of rolling stones and sand which stops only on the Sabbath when it is surrounded by fire and covered by a cloud. In his account Eldad explained how he and a companion of the tribe of Asher embarked on a journey, were shipwrecked, and captured by cannibals. His companions were eaten, but he was rescued by a Jew of the tribe of Issachar. In this report, he also described the ten tribes, their location and existence. By providing such information, he intensified the messianic longing of Jews of the ninth century.

The Crusades and Messianic Expectations

At the end of the eleventh century, Christian Crusaders attacked Jewish communities between the Rhine and the Moselle; cities which were particularly affected included Metz, Speyer, Worms, Mainz, Cologne and Trier. During this pogrom approximately 4000 Jews lost their lives – the horror of this onslaught is recorded in various penitential prayers (*selihot*), lamentations (*kinnot*) and memoirs. Paradoxically, the date of the First Crusade (1096) was viewed by many Jews as the year of their deliverance. Thus the twelfth-century chronicler of the First Crusade, Solomon ben Simeon, stressed the widespread acceptance of this calculation:

> And it came to pass in the year 4856, the 1028th year of our exile, in the eleventh year of the 256th cycle (1096), when we had hoped for salvation and comfort, according to the prophecy of Jeremiah: 'Sing (the Hebrew equivalent of which is 256 according to *gematria* (numerical mystical calculation)) with gladness for Jacob and shout at the head of the nation' (31:7). But it was turned into sorrow and groaning, weeping and lamentation. (in Silver, 1978, 58–9)

Another twelfth-century writer, Eliezer ben Nathan in his report on Jewish persecution during this year emphasized that many Jews viewed the first year of the 256 cycle (1096) as the year of redemption. As he wrote in his *selihah*:

> Time and time again our soul waited
> But the end was long delayed and the wound was not healed;
> In the season of 'Sing' (256 in *gematria*) we hoped that redemption would come.
> But we hoped for peace, and there was none; for a time of healing and behold dismay! (in Silver, 1978, 59)

The general adoption of 1096 as the year for the coming

of the Messiah is also supported by the midrashic commentary of Tobiah ben Eliezer, composed in 1097. Commenting on Exodus 3:20 ('So I will stretch out my hand and smite Egypt with all the wonders which I will do in it; after that he will let you go'), he declared:

> And in the year 4857, that is to say, the year 1029 since the destruction of the Second Temple, which is also the twelfth year in the 256th cycle, I, Tobiah, son of R. Eliezer, looked searchingly into our divine books and considered the length of our exile, how 'their power is gone, and there is none remaining, bond or free' (Deuteronomy 32:36), and how all the ends have passed and redemption is now dependent upon repentance alone, as it is written, 'If you return, O Israel, says the Lord, to me you should return' (Jeremiah 4:1); and again 'If you return, I will restore you, and you shall stand before me' (Jeremiah 15:19). We are now looking to the Rock of our salvation, trusting that even as in the days of Egypt he will now show us wonders. (in Silver, 1978, 59–60)

In another text of this period, Benjamin ben Zerah, who possibly witnessed the First Crusade, recounted taunts delivered by the enemies of Israel about messianic longing such as: 'Ye have calculated the times of redemption and they are now past, and the hope of salvation is over and gone.'

After the tragedy of 1096 the Jewish community began to hope that this disaster was 'the birth pangs of the Messiah'. Hence the twelfth-century scholar Samuel ben Judah in his dirge for the Sabbath before *Shavuot* (which mentions the year 1096) prayed that Jewish suffering might inaugurate the commencement of the messianic age:

> Bring nigh the end of the wonders,
> Deliver thy people from hardship
> Thou, our Redeemer, Lord of Hosts.
> Be thou not quiet, Lord! (in Silver, 1978, 61)

Another writer of this time, David ben Meshullam, ended his lament about the martyrs of the Crusades with an appeal for redemption:

> O living God! Accredit thou to us the merit of their
> blameless lives (the martyrs) and put an end to our
> suffering. (in Silver, 1978, 61)

Again, another figure of this period, David ben Samuel
Halevi wrote in his liturgical prayer (*piyyut*):

> Our soul languishes for thy salvation. When wilt thou
> comfort us?
> Do it for the sake of thy holy name. Not for our sake, O
> Lord, not for our sake. (in Silver, 1978, 61)

The same desire for redemption is found in the writings
of the chroniclers of the Second Crusade which took place
from 1145 to 1147, the Third Crusade which occurred
from 1189 to 1190, as well as other disasters of this age.
Thus Issac ben Shalom concluded his liturgical prayer
about the massacre of the German communities on the
12th Nisan 1147 with a supplication for salvation:

> Have pity upon thy scattered ones, O Holy One,
> And with thy gracious spirit uphold us.
> Arise, our help, deliver us. (in Silver, 1978, 62)

Another Jewish scholar, Ephraim ben Jacob of Bonn who
witnessed the horrors of the Second and Third Crusades,
longed for deliverance after the devastation of the Jewish
community of Blois in 1171. 'How long shall I hope for
redemption at the hands of the sons of David and the
prophet Elijah?', he asked. Likewise Hillel ben Jacob in
his *selihah* on those who were killed in Blois, prayed:

> Accept, I pray thee, my prayer, O God on high!
> Hasten deliverance, and rescue thy poor people.
> Establish thy city and thy dwelling place as of old in beauty
> So that God may dwell in Zion. (in Silver, 1978, 62)

Another poet of this period, Menahem ben Jacob, who
recounted the tragedy of Boppard in 1179 where Jews who
were falsely accused of murdering a Christian woman
were thrown into a river and drowned, similarly pleaded:

And if we be unworthy of redemption,
Remember thy servants (Hananiah, Mishael and Azariah)
who would not defile themselves. (in Silver, 1978, 63)

The Crusades therefore gave rise to widespread longing for the coming of the Messiah. Faced with destruction and massacre, the Jewish people eagerly awaited the Redeemer who would come to save them from their miseries and usher in the period of messianic deliverance.

6

Speculation during the
Middle Ages

At the time of the Crusades, Jewish aspirations for the
advent of the Messiah intensified. As a consequence,
when the massacres of this period occurred, the Jewish
community envisaged this disaster as the birth pangs of
the Messiah. In later years the same desire for redemption
and return to Zion was expressed by Jews who continued
to suffer at the hands of Christians. In the following two
centuries a number of Jewish scholars attempted to ascertain the date of divine deliverance on the basis of texts
from the Book of Daniel; prominent among these writers
was Solomon ibn Gabirol, Rashi, Judah Halevi, and Abraham bar Hiyya. Simultaneously several pseudo-Messiahs
appeared in the Jewish world. Initially such figures came
from Asia Minor, Babylonia and Persia, but with the
movement of Jewry to Mediterranean countries other
would-be Messiahs emerged in Western Europe. The most
important figure of this period was David Alroy who, even
after his death, was viewed by his disciples as the
Redeemer of Israel. In the following centuries messianic
calculators sought to determine the year of deliverance
and return of the exiles to the Holy Land on the basis of
scriptural texts. Often they relied on kabbalistic modes of
exegesis in their computations. Pre-eminent among such
writers were Nahmanides, Isaac ben Judah Halevi, Levi
ben Gershon and Bahya ben Asher. Mystical tracts of this
era such as the *Zohar* also contain speculations about the
Messianic Age. In the thirteenth century another messianic figure appeared; although he attracted a wide

following, he evoked considerable animosity from such scholars as Solomon ben Abraham Adret of Barcelona.

Medieval Calculations

During the eleventh and twelfth centuries various Jewish scholars attempted to determine the date of the advent of the Messiah. The eleventh-century philosopher Solomon ibn Gabirol, for example, is referred to by the twelfth-century exegete Abraham Ibn Ezra in his commentary on Daniel 11:30 as having determined the end on the basis of astrological computations. Even though Ibn Gabirol's own messianic speculations have been lost, his poetry is full of messianic allusions. Hence in one *piyyut* he depicted a dialogue between God and Israel in which Israel complains: 'Thy end is long drawn, and my gloom has lasted long. How long will the exile last? When will the appointed season arrive? When wilt thou resolve what is hidden and sealed?' The answer is given: 'Hope on, hapless one, yet a little while longer!' In another *piyyut* the same consolation is conveyed: 'Hearken now, hapless and pilloried one, hope and wait for me, for very soon will I send my angel to prepare my way' (Davidson, 1923, 22).

Another eleventh-century scholar, Rashi, maintained that Daniel 8:14 ('For two thousand and three hundred evenings and mornings; then the sanctuary shall be restored to its rightful state'), and Daniel 12:11 ('And from the time that the continual burnt offering is taken away, and the abomination that makes desolate is set up, there shall be a thousand two hundred and ninety days'), point to 1352 as the year of redemption. According to the *gematria*, the words 'evening' and 'morning' in Daniel 8:14 = 574. To this should be added the number 2300 mentioned in the same verse. This produces 2874. The *terminus a quo* is the beginning of Egyptian captivity. The ancient Israelites were in captivity in Egypt for 210 years; 480 years elapsed from their deliverance to the establishment of the Temple. The Temple lasted for 410 years. The Babylonian captivity lasted for 70 years. And the

Temple stood for 420 years. This produces a total of 1590 years from the time of the Egyptian captivity to the destruction of the Second Temple, and Daniel 12:11–12 states that 1290 years must elapse from the time that the continual burnt offering is taken away until the deliverance. Rashi stresses that the offering ceased six years before the destruction – in the 1584th year since the Egyptian captivity. Adding 1584 to 1290 makes 2874. The Temple was destroyed in 68 CE. The Messiah will arrive 1290 years after the cessation of the burnt offering – this occurred six years before the destruction (in 62 CE). Rashi therefore believed that the messianic age would commence in 1352.

A contemporary of Rashi, Judah Halevi, encouraged his fellow Jews not to become anxious about the coming of the Messiah. In one of his poems he wrote:

> Let thy heart be strong, awaiting thine appointed season of redemption. Why do you calculate the end of the captivity and grow disturbed? ... Thou hast done well to wait for thy Redeemer. Do not, therefore, be impatient; thou wilt behold the glory of my work. (Davidson, 1923, 25)

Nevertheless, Halevi himself engaged in messianic speculation. In one of his poems he related that he had a dream in which he saw the downfall of Ishmael: 'In the year 1130 all thy pride (Ishmael) will be shattered. Thou wilt be abashed and ashamed of the things which thou didst devise' (Poems I, 57–8). Here he contended that Ishmael is the fourth kingdom mentioned in the Book of Daniel whose destruction would bring about God's redemption: 'Art thou the miry clay in the feet of iron which came at the end and was exalted?' (Poems II, 151). Fixing upon this date, Halevi was following a tradition among Jews in Muslim lands that the Messiah would emerge 500 years after the rise of Islam – in the previous century it was commonly believed that the Messiah would come 400 years after the Hegira (in 1022). The Karaite commentator, Jacob ben Reuben, for example, stated that 'it is likely that the redemption will occur at the end of 400 years of the rule of the little horn (Islam)' (Poems II, 151). When this hope evaporated, the date of deliverance was put forward 100 years. This is illustrated by the statement which Abd al Mumin, head of the Almohades, made to the leader of the Jews of Morocco when he conquered that country: 'I know that your fathers said that your Messiah would come 500 years after the rise of Mohammed, and now the time is past and your Messiah has not yet appeared' (Graetz, IV, 198).

In the same century Abraham bar Hiyya, who was a contemporary of Halevi, also speculated about the coming of the Messianic Age. In his *Megillat ha-Megalleh* he defended such calculation: it was sanctioned by the Torah and practised by leading scholars. According to bar Hiyya, the world was created for the sake of Israel; hence every cycle in the creation account has symbolic significance in the history of the nation. The creation week signifies that the world will endure 6000 years to be followed by a millennial Sabbath. Such an account is based on Psalm 90:4: 'For a thousand years in thy sight are but as yesterday when it is past.' In bar Hiyya's view, a day in God's sight is in fact 857 1/7 years since a watch in the night = 1/3 of the night (4 hours). Thus a day = 6/7 of 1000 years (857 1/7 years). Each day is divided into seven parts, and each part (122 years) = 1 generation. On the basis of this calculation bar Hiyya formulated a number of alternative dates of messianic deliverance. First the flood, he stated, occurred at the close of the second day (1714 AM [= *Anno Mundi*, in the year of the world]); the Torah was given towards the end of the third day 2448 AM). From such calculations it is evident that the next three days will last another 2448 years. As a result the total calculation is 4896 (1136 CE). This is the year of messianic deliverance. Alternatively, as a second calculation, it is possible to reckon that the third day ended at the conquest of Canaan (2495 AM) – this would place the year of messianic redemption at 4990 AM (2495 × 2 = 4990 AM or 1230 CE.

As a third option, it is possible to interpret Deuteronomy 28:63 ('And as the Lord took delight in doing you good and multiplying you, so the Lord will take delight in bringing ruin upon you and destroying you; and you shall be plucked off the land which you are entering to take possession of it') as indicating that the period of suffering will be as long as the time of rejoicing. The period of rejoicing which began with the giving of the Torah (2448 AM) concluded with the destruction (3828 AM) = 1380 years. The period of suffering will last an equal time until 5208 AM. This year, 1148 CE, will therefore be the year of redemption.

A final calculation was based on the assumption that the Torah was given in 2448 AM at the close of the third day. The remaining four days would therefore last 3552 years (approximately 890 years per day). The First Temple was destroyed at the end of the fourth day (3338 AM = 890 years after the giving of the Torah). The fifth and sixth days will last 1780 years (890 × 2). At the close of the sixth day the Messiah will come (1780 + 3338 = 5118 AM or 1358 CE). Thus the advent of the Messiah will take place at this time. This latter calculation is further supported by astrological evidence. According to bar Hiyya, the history of Israel from the time of the Exodus to his own day demonstrates the relative positions of the conjunction of the planets Saturn and Jupiter. The conjunction of these two planets in the sign of Pisces in the watery trigon took place in 2365 AM. This presaged the redemption from Egypt and the giving of the Torah. This same conjunction will not occur again until after 2859 years (or in 5224 AM = 1464 CE). Messianic deliverance will take place in the last of the twelve major conjunctions between 1226 and 1464. Specifically it will occur in the thirteenth year of the seventh minor conjunction of this trigon (1358 CE).

False Messiahs

At the end of the eleventh and throughout the twelfth century a number of pseudo-Messiahs appeared in the Jewish world. In 1096 the arrival of the Crusaders gave rise to widespread excitement among Jews living in the Byzantine empire. As a consequence, the French Jewish community sent a representative to Constantinople to obtain information about the advent of the Messiah. In Khazaria seventeen communities marched to the desert to meet the ten lost tribes. In Salonika the arrival of the prophet Elijah was announced. According to various reports, someone had received Elijah's staff, and another individual had been cured of blindness. As a result, many Jews fasted, prayed and did penance. During this period a proselyte, Obadiah, journeyed to northern Palestine where he encountered the Karaite Solomon Ha-Kohen who declared that he was the Messiah and would soon redeem the Jewish nation. In Mesopotamia another messianic figure, ben Chadd, appeared but was subsequently arrested by the caliph of Baghdad.

In the next century a false messianic forerunner in Yemen was described by the twelfth-century Jewish philosopher Moses Maimonides:

In Yemen there arose a man who said that he was the messenger of the Messiah, preparing the way for his coming. He also announced that the Messiah would appear in Yemen. Many Jews and Arabs followed him. He traversed the country and misled the people, urging them to follow him and to go to meet the Messiah. Our brothers of Yemen wrote to me a long letter informing me about the manner of the man and the innovations which he introduced in the prayers, and what he told them, and reporting also the miracles which he performed, and they solicited my opinion about the matter. I understood from what they wrote that that poor man was ignorant although God-fearing, and that all that men reported concerning his performance was absolutely false.

I feared me for the safety of the Jews living there, and so I composed for them three dissertations ... on the subject of the King-Messiah, and how to know him, and the signs which will usher him in. And I urged upon them to warn that man lest he be lost and lest he also bring destruction upon the (Jewish) communities. The upshot of the matter was that at the end of the year the man was caught and all of his followers deserted him.

An Arab king questioned him, and he replied that he had

spoken the truth and that he had obeyed the word of God. The king asked him for a sign. He replied, 'Cut off my head and I will return to life again.' The king said that there could be no greater sign than that, and if his word came true, he and all the world would believe that he spoke the truth ... The king commanded and they cut off his head, and the poor man was killed. May his death atone for him and for all Israel. The Jews in many communities were heavily fined. To this day there are ignorant men who believe that he will arise from his grave and appear. (in Silver, 1978, 78–9)

Maimonides in his *Iggeret Teman* also referred to other messianic figures of this period. 'And similarly,' he wrote, 'there arose a man in the West in the city of Fez 44 years ago (1127) who said that he was the herald announcing that the Messiah would appear that year. His word did not come true, and because of him persecutions befell Israel. A man who witnessed it all told me about it.' Again, he continued: 'And ten years before this event there arose in Cordoba, Spain a man who boasted that he was the Messiah, and because of him Israel came very near destruction.' Another messianic figure appeared in 1087: 'And thirty years before this time (1087) there arose a man in France who announced that he was the Messiah, and performed signs, according to their opinion, and the French killed him, and many other Jews were slain with him.' (in Silver, 1978, 79)

The most important pseudo-Messiah of this period was David Alroy who appeared in 1147 at the time of the Second Crusade. Born in Amadiya, east of Mosul, his real name was Menahem ben Solomon, but he called himself David due to his claim to be king of the Jews. The name Alroy is a corruption of al-Daji, his Arabic family name. According to tradition, he was educated at the Baghdad academy, learned in mysticism, and skilled in sorcery. The movement to recognize his messiahship probably began among mountain Jews of the north-east Caucasus before 1121, and gathered momentum in the ferment that accompanied the struggles between Christianity and Islam following the First Crusade and during the wars preceding the Second Crusade. The suffering and massacres of this period were perceived by many Jews as the birth pangs of the Messiah. The principal figure of this messianic circle was Solomon, Alroy's father, who claimed to be the prophet Elijah.

The leaders of this messianic sect sought to announce Alroy's Messiahship by addressing a letter 'to all Jews dwelling near-by and far off and in all the surrounding countries'. In their proclamation, they stated: 'The time has come in which the Almighty will gather together his people Israel from every country to Jerusalem the holy city.' In anticipation of this event, they stressed the importance of penitential preparation through fasting and prayer. After opponents of this group protested about such exhortations, the movement was suppressed and Alroy re-established his centre in Amadiya. The strategic position of Amadiya as a Muslim base for operating against Edessa had been strengthened by fortifications built by Zangi, ruler of Mosul. Alroy was encouraged in his activities by Muslim sectarians (Yezidis) who also sought to gain control of the stronghold. Rumours were then circulated that when Alroy was imprisoned by the Seljuk sultan, the overlord of the area, he had magically escaped. Alroy then besought other Jews from the vicinity as well as those living in Azerbaijan, Persia, and the Mosul region to join his entourage – they were to come with weapons concealed in their garments to observe how he would obtain control of the city.

A contemporary, Benjamin of Tudela, depicted this messianic movement in his itinerary:

> He (David Alroy) took it into his head to revolt against the king of Persia, and to gather around him the Jews who lived in the mountains of Chaftan, in order to war against the gentiles and to capture Jerusalem. He showed miraculous signs to the Jews, and declared that God sent him to capture Jerusalem and to lead them forth from among the nations, and the people believed in him and proclaimed him the Messiah. (in Silver, 1978, 80)

Tradition relates that two impostors forged a letter allegedly from Alroy in which he promised to transport Jews of Baghdad to Jerusalem by night on the wings of angels. When this even failed to materialize, his pretensions were ridiculed. Eventually he was murdered, possibly by his father-in-law who was bribed by the governor of Amadiya. Nonetheless, a number of his followers – the Menahem-ites – continued to believe in him after his death.

Messianism in the Thirteenth and Fourteenth Centuries

Even though messianic predictions during the eleventh and twelfth centuries failed to materialize, speculation about the coming of the Messiah continued to preoccupy Jewish thinkers. The hope of deliverance from suffering and persecution encouraged Jewish thinkers to compute the date of divine deliverance. Influenced by mystical thought, these scholars increasingly relied on kabbalistic theories to determine when redemption would take place. Pre-eminent among these writers of the thirteenth century was the theologian and mystic Nahmanides. In his *Book of Redemption*, he sought to harmonize dates in the Book of Daniel and deduce from them the year of the Messiah's arrival. In his view, Daniel 12:11 ('And from the time that the continual burnt offering is taken away, and the abomination that makes desolate is set up, there shall be a thousand two hundred and ninety days') implies that 1290 years after the destruction of the Temple the Messiah ben Joseph will emerge. To substantiate this interpretation, Nahmanides employed several *gematriot*: Genesis 15:13 ('They will be oppressed for four hundred years') – the *gematria* here is 1293; Deuteronomy 4:30 ('When you are in tribulation, and all these things come upon you in the latter days') – the *gematria* in this verse is 1291. In both cases the number of years between destruction and redemption is approximately 1290.

Again, with reference to Daniel 12:11, he maintained that the burnt offering was taken away on the day of destruction – 45 years later the Messiah ben David will arrive. This accounts for the figure of 1335 in the next verse: 'Blessed is he who waits and comes to the thousand three hundred and thirty-five days' (Daniel 12:12). This figure, 1335 years, helps to account for the numbers in Daniel 8:14: 'For two thousand and three hundred evenings and mornings; then the sanctuary shall be restored to its rightful state.' Here 2300 refers to the number of years which will elapse from David's reign until the termination of the exile: David's reign (40 years) + the duration of the First Temple (410 years) + the Babylonian captivity (70 years) + the duration of the Second Temple (420 years) + the duration of the last exile (1335) = 2275 (approximately 2300 years).

These verses in Daniel therefore illustrate that the duration of the last exile will be 1335 years; at this point in time the advent of the Messiah ben David will take place. In what year will this occur? Nahmanides stated in a public disputation with Pablo Christiani in 1263 CE: 'It is now 1195 years since the destruction, or 95 years less than the messianic figure of Daniel (1195 + 95 = 1290). We believe that the Messiah will come that year.' This means that the Messiah ben Joseph will arrive in 1358 (1263 + 95 = 1358). Forty-five years later, 1403, the Messiah ben David will appear (1263 + 95 + 45 = 1403) – this calculation is based on the second figure of 1335 days in Daniel 12:13 (1195 + 95 + 45).

Another scholar of this period, Issac ben Judah Halevi, in his commentary on the Pentateuch, quoted the author of the biblical commentary *Gan* as indicating that Deuteronomy 28:63 ('And as the Lord took delight in doing you good and multiplying you, so the Lord will take delight in bringing ruin upon you and destroying you') contains a messianic prediction. This verse is to be combined with Daniel 12:11 ('And from the time that the continual burnt offering is taken away ... there shall be a thousand two hundred and ninety days'). These verses, he argued, imply that the exile will last as long as the period of rejoicing. The period of rejoicing lasted from the sojourn in Egypt to the destruction of the First Temple (1290 years); hence the exile will last 1290 years. The number 1335 in the following verse in Daniel (Daniel 12:12) refers to the conquest of the world by the Messiah which will happen 45 years after his appearance.

However, it is impossible to predict with certainty when this period begins and ends. 'We do not know when the period of 1290 years begins', he wrote, 'or we would know exactly when it will end ... it may begin with the taking away of the continual burnt offering in the days of Hyrcan and Aristobulus ... or it may begin with the reign of Herod, who was not fit to be king over Israel, or perhaps at an even later date, i.e. with the expulsion. At the time of the end when the Messiah will come ... it shall become clear when the period actually began' (in Silver, 1978, 86).

In the fourteenth century the Jewish philosopher, Levi ben Gershon, also found evidence of messianic redemption in the final chapter of the Book of Daniel. On the basis of Daniel 12:11, he maintained that 1290 years will elapse from the destruction to the redemption. Since the destruction took place in 3828 AM, messianic deliverance will occur in 5118 AM (1358 CE). The number 1335 in the following verse (Daniel 12:12), 45 years later, refers to the end of the messianic war against Gog and Magog (1403 CE).

Another writer of this period, Bahya ben Asher, formulated messianic calculations in his commentary on the Torah where he points out that the Bible gives three numbers for the duration of the Egyptian exile – 210, 400, and 430 years. The duration of the present exile will also have three figures: 1150 (Daniel 8:14) (2300 mornings and evenings = 1150 days); 1290 (Daniel 12:11); and 1335 (Daniel 12:12). Thus, if Israel is unworthy to be delivered after 1150 years (1218 CE), redemption will take place after 1290 years (1358 CE). Alternatively, if Israel continues to be unworthy, messianic redemption will not occur until after 1335 years (1403 CE). To this computation, Bahya added another based on the conviction that the seven days of creation and rest indicate the seven millennia of the earth's existence and final destruction.

The first day, he argued, symbolizes the fifth millennium (the period of exile); the sixth day is symbolic of the sixth millennium when the Messiah will come. In his commentary composed in 1291, he stated that his generation is in the 51st year of that millennium. In Bahya's view, the Messiah will arrive after the end of the first tenth of the millennium (in 5118 AM or 1358 CE). The figure 1335 in Daniel 12:12, – 45 day-years later – refers to the close of the period of the wars which the Messiah's coming will bring about (1403 CE).

In addition to these calculations, a number of kabbalistic texts from this period contain speculation about the coming of the Messiah. The *Zohar*, for example, provides a number of messianic dates based on mystical computations. One calculation is based on the mystical value of God's name (*yod, he, vav, he*). When Israel went into exile, the last letters of his name were separated. The letter *he* symbolizes 5000 years; the *vav* 6000 years. When the fifth millennium will end and the sixth begin, these letters will be joined: this will occur in the sixtieth year of the sixth millennium (5060 AM = 1300 CE). Thus 1300 CE is the date of messianic redemption. Another calculation, based on the mystic numerical value of the letter *vav* (6) sets the date as 1306 CE. The *vav* in the name Jacob in the verse 'I will remember my covenant with Jacob' (Leviticus 26:42) is the key to this calculation. The act of remembrance will take place in the sixtieth year of the sixth millennium (1300 CE). In the sixty-sixth year of the sixth millennium, the Messiah will arrive. Yet another calculation is based on the 12 tribes who represent 1200 years. Twelve hundred years after the destruction of the Temple (1268 CE), the night will darken on Israel. This darkness will last for 66 years (1334 CE). At the culmination of this period, the Messiah will appear and engage in warfare. Sixty-six years later (1400 CE), the letters of God's name will appear inscribed in the lower and higher perfection; 132 years later (1532 CE), the resurrection will take place in Palestine; 144 years later (1676 CE), the dead in other lands will be resurrected.

Abraham Abulafia

The most important messianic figure of the thirteenth century was Abraham Abulafia, who announced himself as the Messiah. When a child, his parents moved from Saragossa to Tudela in Navarre. When he was eighteen his father died, and Abulafia subsequently travelled to Palestine where he searched for the mystical river Sambatyon where the ten tribes were believed to reside. Returning by way of Greece, he sojourned in Capua where he studied Maimonides' *Guide of the Perplexed* under Hillel ben Samuel of Verona. In addition, he was introduced to kabbalistic thought by Baruch Togarmi who composed a commentary on the *Sefer Yetzirah*. In 1271 he studied Maimonides' work in Barcelona, became convinced that he had attained prophetic inspiration, and declared his mystical doctrine to a small circle of followers. In 1273 he travelled through Italy, Sicily and Greece, and also wrote a number of mystical essays combining kabbalistic ideas and Maimonides' philosophy. In 1277 he lived in Patras in Greece where he wrote a series of mystical tracts. Three years later he attracted a large circle of followers in Capua.

In 1280 Abulafia went to Rome in an effort to persuade Pope Nicholas III to ameliorate the condition of the Jewish people. When he arrived, the Pope sentenced him to death by burning but because of the Pope's death, this decree was not carried out. After a month in prison, Abulafia was released and went to Sicily. In Messina he wrote *Or ha-Sekhel* about the mysteries of God's name. Here he declared that the onset of the messianic era would take place in 1290; many were persuaded and prepared to leave for Palestine. Yet despite such a favourable response, his teachings aroused great hostility. As a result, his opponents approached Solomon ben Abraham Adret of Barcelona, accusing Abulafia of claiming to be the Messiah. In response, Adret called Abulafia a scoundrel: Abulafia was compelled to flee to the island of Comino where he composed polemical treatises in which he defended himself and his views.

Abulafia's mystical ideas were based on the doctrine of the ten *sefirot* (divine emanations) and utilized the methods of *zeruf* (combination of letters), *gematria* (numerical value of Hebrew words), and *notarikon* (letters of a word as abbreviation of sentences). Believing prophetic *kabbalah* enabled human beings to have prophetic powers and commune with God, he argued that human reason can become subject to the rule of divine universal reason. This process he called the 'Way of the Divine Name'. In the *Book of the Sign*, he argues that through the technique of combining the letters of various divine names, one can receive an outpouring of the Holy Spirit and thereby attain prophetic illumination:

> Prophecy is a mode of the intellect. It is the expression of the love of the Lord our God, the Lord is One ... Here is the strong foundation which I deliver to you that you should know it and engrave it upon your heart: The Holy Name, the whole of the Torah, the sacred Scriptures and all the prophetic books; these are all full of divine names and tremendous things. Join one to the other. Depict them to yourself. Test them, try them, combine them ... First begin by combining the letters of the name YHVH. Gaze at all its combinations. Elevate it. Turn it over like a wheel that goes round and round, backwards and forwards like a scroll. Do not set it aside except when you observe that it is becoming too much for you because of the confused movements in your imagination. Leave it for a while and you will be able to return to it later. You can then make your request of it and when you attain to wisdom do not forsake it.
>
> For the initial letters and the final letters, the numerical values, the *notarikons*, the combinations of letters and the permutations, their accents and the forms they assume, the knowledge of their names and the grasping of their ideas, the changing of many words into one and one into many – all these belong to the authentic tradition of the prophets ... We know by a prophetic divine tradition of the Torah that when the sage who is an adept combines (the letters of the divine name) one with the other, the holy spirit flows into him. When you look at these holy letters in truth and reliance and when you combine them – placing that which is at the beginning at the end and that which is at the end at the

beginning, and that which is in the middle at the end and so forth in like manner – these letters will all roll backwards and forwards with many melodies.

Let him begin gently and then make haste. Let him train himself to be thoroughly familiar with the changes as they are combined, and it is essential, too, for him to be thoroughly familiar with the secrets of the Torah and the wisdom thereof in order to know that which he brings about through these combinations. Let him awaken his heart to reflect on the spiritual, divine, prophetic picture. (Jacobs, 1977, 57–61)

Believing he had such knowledge of the mystery of the alphabet and numbers, Abulafia was persuaded that he could attain the heights of revelation. 'But when I reached to the Names and untied the seal bands,' he stated, 'the Lord of all revealed himself to me and made known to me his secret, and informed me concerning the end of the exile and the beginning of the redemption through the blood avenger.' By understanding the mystery of letters, vowels, numerals and God's name, it became possible for Abulafia to exercise miraculous powers. In his view, Israel suffers in exile, because it has forgotten God's true name; only by means of such knowledge which Abulafia possessed will the redemption occur. Hence Abulafia's mystical role was determined by such esoteric mystical comprehension of the divine mysteries. In all likelihood the rumours of his messiahship contributed to the emigration of Jews, headed by Rabbi Meir of Rothenburg, for Palestine in 1286.

A number of Abulafia's disciples continued his prophecies and predictions after his death. In Avila one of his followers, Abraham of Avila, declared that the advent of the Messiah would take place on the last day of the fourth month in the year 1295. Such a prediction persuaded the Jewish community there to await the appointed day with anticipation. Yet when this event failed to materialize, those residents who had assembled in the synagogues were profoundly discouraged. Attentive to this state of affairs, Adret emphasized that proper precautions should be taken when confronted by a messianic pretender. In every case, the prophecies of such a would-be Messiah must be scrutinized, and his character, conduct and motives should be investigated with care.

7

Messianism during the Early Modern Period

Despite the failure of the Messiah to appear in 1348 and 1403, the Jewish community continued to await the advent of the messianic age. As a consequence, these centuries witnessed the composition of messianic treatises and such scholars as Simeon ben Duran and Isaac Abrabanel speculated about the year of his arrival. This tradition of messianic calculation was practised in the next century by scholars including Abraham Halevi, Mordecai ben Jacob Dato, Isaac Luria, Naphtali Herz ben Jacob Elhanan, Gedalia ibn Yahya and David ben Solomon ibn Abi Zimra. In addition, a number of false Messiahs including David Reuveni and Solomon Molko appeared, claiming to usher in the period of deliverance. Undaunted by the failure of these would-be Messiahs to lead the Jewish people to the Promised Land and bring about redemption, other calculators persisted in their investigations. Pre-eminent among these messianic speculators was Hayyim Vital, the disciple of Issac Luria who announced that he was the Messiah ben Joseph. Another major figure of this period was Manasseh ben Israel who maintained that the hour of redemption was at hand. Convinced that this momentous event was about to take place, he sought to persuade Oliver Cromwell to admit the Jews to England. Eventually the Cossack Rebellion which began in 1648 and devastated Polish Jewry heightened the expectation that the coming of the Messiah was close at hand.

Messianic Calculators in the Fourteenth and Fifteenth Centuries

The failure of the Messiah to arrive in 1348 and 1403 was a terrible blow to the Jewish community, discouraging further speculation. Instead of divine redemption, the fourteenth century brought about further tragedies to the Jewish population. Nevertheless, there did appear a number of rabbinic treatises on the coming of the Messiah in the latter part of the fourteenth century as well as in the fifteenth century. The *Book of the Alphabet*, for example, is a mystical tract on the Hebrew alphabet in which the author calculates that the Messiah will arrive in 1430 on the basis of *gematria* and *notarikon*. In another treatise of this period, *Sefer ha-Pelia'ah we-ha-Kanah*, composed in the fifteenth century by a Sephardi kabbalist, the date of 1490 is given as the year of deliverance on the basis of mystical computations.

Distinguished scholars of this period such as Simeon ben Zemah Duran also predicted the arrival of the Messiah. In his commentary on the Book of Job, he determined that the Messiah would appear in 1850. This computation was based on an allegorical interpretation of Job 40:41. In defence of this view, he also cited Ezekiel 4:4ff. An interpretation of this passage gives rise to the number 2450 years. Here Duran maintained that 150 years elapsed from the expulsion of some of the tribes of the Northern Kingdom under Tiglath-Pileser to the expulsion under Sennacherib. This accounts for the discrepancy in the two revelations in Daniel 12:7 and 8:14. According to Duran, the first text provides the figure 2450, and the second 2300. Assuming Duran's starting point to have been the final destruction of the Kingdom of Israel – which according to the old chronology was c. 450 BCE – then the redemption will occur 2300 years later = 1850 CE. Duran further argued that the figure in Daniel 2:11 (1290) refers to the conquest of Jerusalem by the Muslims. For Duran, the end of Islamic rule will take place 1290 years after the rise of Muhammad 622 + 1290 = 1912 CE. The beginning of the end would take place 60 years earlier (c. 1850 CE).

During the fourteenth century the pseudo-Messiah Moses Botarel appeared. A scholar and kabbalist, he declared himself to be the Messiah in 1393 after widespread persecution in Spain which was generally viewed by the Jewish community as the birth pangs of the Messiah. As Abraham of Granada stated in *Berit Menuha*:

> And this is an indication of the approach of redemption. When it is near, the sufferings of the exile will increase, and many of the faithful ones will stumble when they see the terrible confusion of the exile and the great sufferings, and many will leave the faith in order to escape the sword of the destroyer ... but blessed is the man who will cling to his faith and walk in the right path. Perhaps he will be saved from the tribulations which are called the pangs of the Messiah. (in Silver, 1978, 109)

Not only was Botarel accepted as the Messiah by the general population, but also scholars such as Hasdai Crescas appeared to have believed in his claims as well.

The events of the next century led to further speculation about the coming of the messianic age. The expulsions of the Jews from Spain in 1492, from Portugal in 1498, and from Germanic provinces in the last decades of the fifteenth century intensified Jewish longings for a return to the Promised Land. The most important messianic treatise of this period was by the sixteenth-century thinker Isaac Abrabanel whose *Wells of Salvation* is a treatise on the Book of Daniel in which he seeks to ascertain the date of deliverance.

In the first section, he explained that the prohibition against calculating the advent of the Messiah applies only to those who use astrological computations, but not to those who interpret Scripture correctly. 'Our life is so hard,' he wrote, 'and our fortunes so unhappy that we are constrained to inquire after the hour of our release and redemption. Furthermore, the end is not far off, and it is now proper to reveal it' (in Silver, 1978, 117). In the next section, he maintained that the fourth kingdom referred to in Daniel is Rome, and that the vision of the Chariot in Ezekiel is messianic in character: the 'four living creatures and the four wheels' refer to the four kingdoms. He then explained the motivation of messianic prophecies. They were made, he stated, to proclaim the power of God and draw human beings to repentance. Salvation is the reward for the righteous, and the prophet therefore declares that redemption will be vouchsafed to those who trust in God whereas those who sin will be punished.

After these observations, Abrabanel offered a running commentary on the Book of Daniel – here he discussed Nebuchadnezzar's dream and Daniel's interpretation. The land of gold, he stated, is Babylon; the breast and arms of silver are Persia; the belly and thighs of brass, Greece; the legs of iron, Rome; the feet (part iron and part clay) refer to Christianity and Islam which divided the Roman world. The fifth kingdom is Israel, and the one who shatters the feet of iron is the Messiah. This discussion is followed by Abrabanel's exegesis of the dream in Daniel 7: the first beast, which is compared to a lion, is Babylon; the second beast, likened to a bear, is Persia; the third beast, likened to a leopard, is Greece, and the fourth beast is Rome. The fifth beast, he stated, will be destroyed because of the teaching of the papacy. Eventually the Messiah will come after a period of great suffering and Israel will endure forever.

The fourth kingdom will endure for 'a time two times and half a time' (Daniel 7:25). A 'time', he stated, is the period of the duration of the First Temple (410 years): three and a half times = 1435 years. This figure, which dates from the year of the destruction (68 CE), = 1503. This date, 1503 CE, is therefore the time when the Messiah will arrive (or the preliminary events – the destruction of Rome and the punishment of the gentiles – will take place). Such a calculation is further supported by the account of Daniel's second vision in Daniel 8. The ram Daniel witnessed is Persia; the two horns of the ram are Persia and Media (or Darius the Mede and Cyrus the Persian); the he-goat which smote the ram is Greece; and the conspicuous horn which was between his eyes was Alexander. The four horns are the four parts into which Alexander's empire was divided. The little horn which came out of one is Antiochus Epiphanes. The host in whose hands the continual offering was given over due to the sins of the nation is Titus. The two holy ones are the angels Michael and Gabriel. The 2300 evenings and mornings – the duration of the exile – are 2300 years which are to be counted from the division of the kingdom which took place in 2965 AM. Adding 2300 + 2965 = 5265 AM or 1504 (c. 1503 CE).

In Abrabanel's second book, the *Salvation of His Anointed*, he sought to refute Jewish apostates who sought to prove that the Messiah had already come. The Talmud appears to contain messianic calculations which point to a previous date; further, there are some rabbis who appear to have believed that the Messiah will never come. In this treatise, Abrabanel sought to show that these texts do not in fact deny the ultimate appearance of the Messiah, nor do the talmudic dates suggest that the Messiah has already come. In a final study, *Announcing Salvation*, Abrabanel attempted to refute those who construed the messianic prophecies in Scripture as applying to the first restoration. In addition, he wished to contradict the belief that the coming of the Messiah is not based on the Bible.

Calculation in the Sixteenth Century

Messianic calculation continued into the sixteenth century with the writings of the Spanish mystic and kabbalist Abraham Halevi; in his work he predicted that the Messianic Age would dawn in 1530. His tract on the Book of Daniel was completed in 1508 in Seres, Greece and published in Constantinople two years later. At the outset of this work, he stated that his computations are the result of logical deduction and are thus subject to error. Nonetheless, he was convinced the messianic period began with the conquest of Constantinople by the Turks in 1453. This victory, he argued, will be followed by the fall of Rome.

The authority he cited for this claim is the Targum of
Jonathan ben Uzziel on Lamentations 4:21 and Obadiah
1:20: 'The exiles in Halah who are of the people of Israel
shall possess Phoenicia as far as Zarephath; and the exiles
of Jerusalem who are in Sepharad shall possess the cities
of the Negeb' (i.e. Palestine). In Halevi's view, Jews are
now living in the final hour of exile. This calculation is
based on Daniel 12:11 where the figure 1290 is mentioned. According to Halevi, this period should not be
reckoned from the destruction (3828 CE), but from
4000 AM. Hence the Messiah will come in 5290 AM (4000 +
1290) or 1530 CE.

Another figure of this period was Solomon Molko, a
sixteenth-century kabbalist, mystic and pseudo-Messiah.
Born in Lisbon of Marrano parents, he was originally
called Diogo Pires. Although little is known of his early
life, he received a secular education and became secretary
to the king's council and recorder at the court of appeals
at the age of 21. After meeting David Reuveni when he
arrived in Portugal in 1525, he asked to be circumcised.
However, when Reuveni refused to perform this act, he
circumcised himself and adopted a Hebrew name. Eventually Reuveni was compelled to leave Portugal because he
was suspected of being involved in Molko's conversion
and he suggested to Molko that he flee as well. Even
though details of Molko's departure are unclear, Reuveni
subsequently asserted that he had sent Molko on a secret
mission to Turkey. Molko himself stated that he received a
divine communication which dictated his departure.

After travelling to various lands he settled in Salonika
for some time where he studied *kabbalah* and gathered
followers who encouraged him to publish a collection of
his sermons about messianic deliverance. When Rome was
sacked in 1527, Molko believed he saw the signs of
impending redemption. In 1529 he returned to Italy
where he preached about the coming of the Messiah.
When an informer revealed that he was a Marrano who
had reverted to the Jewish faith, Molko fled to Pesaro and
later to Rome. By this time he was convinced he was the

Messiah. To fulfil the talmudic legend about the suffering of the Messiah, he dressed as a beggar and sat for thirty days, fasting among the sick on a bridge over the Tiber river near the pope's palace.

In time Pope Clement VII granted Molko protection, and he preached extensively. By 1530 he left Rome for Venice where he met with Reuveni. When he sought to mediate in a dispute involving Jacob Mantino, the pope's physician, Molko aroused the hatred of Mantino and escaped to Rome. Nonetheless, Molko was accused by an inquisitional court of judaizing and condemned to be burned at the stake. The pope, however, intervened on his behalf, and he was saved. In 1531 Molko travelled to northern Italy where he again met Reuveni, and together they went on a mission to Emperor Charles V. According to Rabbi Joselmann of Rosheim, Molko came in order to arouse the emperor to enlist the Jewish community to fight against the Turks. However, instead the emperor brought Molko to Mantua where he was burned at the stake in 1532 for refusing to embrace Christianity. After his death, many of his disciples refused to accept that he had died and remained loyal to the belief that he was the long-awaited Messiah.

In his writings Molko utilized *gematria* in determining that the messianic year would take place in 5300 AM or 1540 CE. At the end of his messianic work, *Sepher ha-Mefoar,* he claimed: 'I have no permission to reveal that which is hidden, but our deliverance is near at hand and will be revealed to all soon in our own days' (in Silver, 1978, 134). Again, in a letter to his friends, he paraphrased Proverbs 3:2–18 as prophetic of the history of Israel, arguing that the present time is the period of divine love in which the Lord is about to fulfil his promise of deliverance as stated in Jeremiah 31:3 ('I have loved you with an everlasting love; therefore I have continued my faithfulness to you').

The Italian rabbi and kabbalist Mordecai ben Judah Dato believed that the Messiah would arrive in 1575. In the words of his contemporary Azariah dei Rossi: 'And more particularly do we know that a famed kabbalist and scholar, Mordecai Dato, wrote a special book named after his brother, *Migdal David*, in which he convincingly proved that the great hope of Israel for the beginning of redemption and the building of the Temple will be fulfilled in the year 1575' (in Silver, 1978, 135). It seems that this date was viewed by many scholars as the year of messianic redemption. Thus dei Rossi stated: 'I am aware of a whole group of the "sons of prophets" who are waiting for the year 1575 as the day of God, in which God will lead forth his people in joy to everlasting salvation' (in Silver, 1978, 136). Such a view was based on the figure 1335 in Daniel 12:12; this was counted from the year 4000 AM (4000 + 1335 = 5335 AM or 1575 CE).

The sixteenth-century kabbalist Isaac Luria also appears to have expected the Messiah to arrive in 1575. According to the narrative of Solomon Shelemiel ben Hayyim composed in 1609:

> At one time near to the hour of his death, we stood with our master Luria by the tomb of Shemaya and Abtalion in Giscala, which is three miles distant from Safed, and he said to us that Shemaya and Abtalion had told him that we should pray that the Messiah ben Joseph should not die. But we did not understand and we did not inquire further ... It was not long before our master was summoned on high. It was then that we understood that he spoke of himself, and that he was the first Messiah ben Joseph, whose sole mission on earth was to bring about the redemption and fill the whole earth with the messianic kingdom. (in Silver, 1978, 137–8)

At another time Luria asked his followers if they would accompany him to Jerusalem on the Sabbath. When they hesitated, he declared: 'Woe unto us that we have not proved worthy to be redeemed. Had you promptly and unanimously replied that you were ready to go, Israel would have then and there been redeemed. For the hour had come, but you were not ready' (in Silver, 1978, 138).

At the end of the sixteenth century Naphtali Herz ben Jacob Elhanan, a German kabbalist and disciple of Luria, composed a mystical treatise in which he stated that Isaac

Luria was the Messiah ben Joseph. If Luria had lived two years longer, he declared, he would have inaugurated the messianic era. But because the age was not worthy, he died after two years' sojourn in Palestine. The year 1475 was a time of grace; since that year God raises up a righteous person in each generation who could become the Messiah if the nation merited redemption.

A further figure of this period, Gedalia ibn Yahya, suggested 1598 as the year of messianic deliverance:

> But I, though young, have bethought me to tell you in connection with this matter (the messianic calculation) what occurred to me, and I swear to you that my words are true. On the night of the seventh day of Passover in the year 1555, being unable to sleep, I began to reflect on how long it will be to the end of the wonders. After a long time I fell asleep, but in the morning, behold, there was an olive leaf in my mouth. The verse 'I see him, but not now' (Numbers 24:17) came to my mind. I found that the numerical value of the entire verse is 5358. Actually the value of the verse is 5312, which is equal to the *gematria* of the letters *he, shin, yod, bet,* suggesting the verse 'he has turned back my wrath from the people of Israel' (Numbers 25:11). Add to this figure the number of letters in Numbers 24:17 from the words 'a star shall come forth' to the end of the verse = 46 and you have the 5358, or 1598 CE. (in Silver, 1978, 140)

Again, David ben Solomon ibn Abi Zimra maintained on the basis of *gematria* that the messianic age will occur 600 years before the close of the sixth millennium (5400 AM or 1640 CE). Even though the sins of the people may delay the arrival of the Messiah, he will come during this time. A later date was advanced by Samuel ben Judah Velerio in the second half of the sixteenth century in his commentary on the Book of Daniel. Here he argued that the time of exile will be 1800 years. (In Daniel 7:25 'time' = 400 years; 'times' = 800 years; 'half a time' = 600 years (400 + 800/2) = 400 + 800 + 600 = 1800). The Second Temple was destroyed in 3828 AM – the end of the present exile will therefore take place in 5628 AM (3828 + 1800) or 1868 CE. An even later date was given by Joseph ben David ibn Yahya who wrote a commentary on Daniel. The prophecy in Daniel 8:14, he maintained, which contains the figure 2300, was given during the reign of Cyrus in 3391 AM. Messianic redemption will therefore take place 2300 years later in 5691 AM (or 1931 CE).

Sixteenth-Century Messianic Expectations

At the beginning of the sixteenth century the German Jew Asher Lämmlein appeared in Isphia near Venice; there he proclaimed that the Messiah will come in 1502. In his *Tzemah David*, David Gans described Lämmlein's claim:

> In the year 1502 Rabbi Lämmlein announced the advent of the Messiah, and throughout the dispersion of Israel his words were credited. Even among the gentiles the news spread, and many believed him. My grandfather, Seligman Ganz smashed his oven in which he baked the *matzot*, being firmly convinced that the next year he would bake his *matzot* in the Holy Land. And I heard from my old teacher, Rabbi Eliezer Trivash, of Frankfurt, that the matter was not without basis, but that he (Lämmlein) had shown signs and proofs, but that perhaps because of our sins was the coming of the Messiah delayed. (in Silver, 1978, 144)

During this epoch, the adventurer David Reuveni aroused messianic expectations. The main sources for knowledge of his activity are his diary and the letters of his contemporaries. Although his real name is unknown, he claimed to be the son of a King Solomon and the brother of a King Joseph who ruled the lost tribes of Reuben, Gad and half Manasseh in the desert of Habor. For this reason he was called 'Reuveni'. On other occasions, he claimed descent from the tribe of Judah and even compiled a pedigree tracing his descent from King David. Although scholars disagree about his origin, it may be that he was a Falasha.

Reuveni's diary provides a description of his travels in the East before his appearance in Europe, yet it is likely

that this account is fictitious. In any event, it is con-
jectured that he was captured and sold as a slave to Arabs
who brought him to Alexandria where he was redeemed
by his co-religionists. After a short sojourn there, he went
to Jerusalem where he encountered the *nagid* Isaac Shu-
lal. He then travelled to Safed where he proclaimed that
he was a Reubenite sent on a mission to Jersualem by the
king of the lost tribes of Israel; his aim was to hasten the
redemption by removing a stone from the Western Wall.
It is claimed that he did this in the presence of the *nagid*,
but subsequently this was denied. He later went to Damascus where he continued to raise messianic expectations;
later he returned to Alexandria and then sailed for
Venice.

In 1523 he appeared in Venice at the age of about 40.
There he declared he was the commander in chief of his
brother's army and he besought Venetian Jews to aid him
on a mission to the pope. Although most Jews were
sceptical of his story, he gained support from a number of
notables including the artist Moses da Castellazzo. In
February of the next year, he arrived in Rome riding a
white horse. There he was received by the humanist
Cardinal Egidio da Viterbo whose support strengthened
Reuveni's position among the Jews of Rome. Later he was
received by Pope Clement VII to whom he proposed a
treaty between his state and the Christian world against
the Muslim population, possibly mentioning the commer-
cial advantages of such a transaction.

To facilitate this measure, Reuveni asked the pope to
give him letters to the Holy Roman emperor Charles V
and Francis I of France, requesting that they help him in
this venture through the supply of armaments. In addition, he asked for a letter to the mythical 'Prester John' in
Ethiopia. Despite Clement's desire for an anti-Turkish
alliance, it was only a year later that he gave him two
letters – one to the king of Portugal and the other to the
Ethiopian king. While in Rome Reuveni gained the support of a number of enlightened Jews including the
bankers Daniel and Vitale da Pisa and Benvenida

Abravanel, the wife of Samuel Abravanel, who sent him money as well as a silk banner embroidered with the Ten Commandments.

From 1525 to 1527 Reuveni lived in Portugal where King John II received him in the style of an official ambassador. Among the Maranno community he was convinced he was the herald of the Messiah, and he declared to the representative of the sultan of Fez that the time had come for Jews to liberate the Holy Land from the Muslims. He also established contact with Jews in North Africa, sending them letters of encouragement. Despite such a reception, his claims brought about considerable unrest and suspicion at court. Summoned by the king, he was accused of attempting to persuade Marranos to return to their ancient tradition. When Diego Pires (Solomon Molko) declared he was a Jew, Reuveni was ordered to leave Portugal, much to the despair of the Marrano community. On his departure he encouraged these Jews to remain faithful: he had come to declare their imminent deliverance.

For a short time Reuveni was shipwrecked off the coast of Provence, and then imprisoned for two years. Finally he was released at the request of the king of France on the payment of a ransom by the Avignon and Carpentras communities. In 1530 he returned to Venice after visiting several places in Italy; there he sought to engage in consultations with the city governors to bring his plans to the attention of the emperor. Again, he evoked messianic longing among the Jewish community. At the suggestion of Frederick, Marquis of Mantua, he was encouraged to reside in Mantua. However, Reuveni's enemies among the Jews charged that Reuveni had forged a series of letters that he had previously lost on his travels. In response, Frederick warned the pope and Charles V when Reuveni and Solomon Molko appeared before the emperor in 1532. There they were imprisoned, and Molko was burned at the stake. Reuveni was taken to Spain in chains where he was charged with seducing new Christians back to the Jewish faith and put to death.

Messianic Expectations in the Seventeenth Century

During the seventeenth century Hayyim Vital, the disciple and interpreter of Isaac Luria, announced that he was the Messiah ben Joseph. Even though he had not set a specific year for the advent of the messianic age, Vital stated that the Messiah would come during his lifetime:

> In the year 1553 a man from Persia, whose name was Rabbi Shaltiel Alshaikh, who sees visions in his waking state, a wise and pious man, who fasts daily, told me that he was continually being informed (by visions) that the redemption of Israel depends upon me (Vital) through my causing Israel to repent, and they also informed him concerning my excellence; and unto this very year (1610) he is still writing me letters about his visions regarding myself and the redemption which is dependant upon me. (in Silver, 1978, 184)

At about the same time he also recounted that a certain Rabbi Sagura visited a magician and fortune-teller to ask about messianic redemption and was told that Israel's lack of repentance delayed the coming of the Messiah. Yet, if the Jewish people would listen to Hayyim Vital, they would be rewarded; on the other hand, much suffering would befall them if they did not hearken to his message.

Another figure of this period, Isaiah Horowitz stressed that the study of the *Zohar* was mandatory. 'Those who study *kabbalah*,' he declared, 'are tenfold more exalted than those who study the Bible and *Mishnah*' (in Silver, 1978, 185). This mystical text was hidden purposely – it will not be revealed until the end of time. Previously it was with the angels for their edification, but with the approach of the messianic era it was revealed to human beings in order that they would engage in its study and receive the merit accruing from this activity: this would hasten the coming of the Messiah. Referring to the calculations in *Midrash ha-Neelam* where the biblical phrase 'In this year of jubilee each of you shall return to his property' is adduced to demonstrate the year of redemption, Horowitz argued this would take place in 1648. The seventeenth-century scholar Yom-Tob Lipmann

Heller in his commentary on *Avot* also seems to adopt this date as the year of messianic deliverance, as did many other writers of this period.

Pre-eminent among the messianic speculators of the seventeenth century was Manasseh ben Israel who was persuaded that the hour of redemption was near at hand, awaiting the complete dispersion of the Jewish people throughout the world. On the basis of this belief, he petitioned Oliver Cromwell to readmit the Jews into England. Thus in his *Vindiciae Judaeorum*, he wrote: 'For I conceived that our universal dispersion was a necessary circumstance to be fulfilled before all that shall be accomplished which the Lord hath promised to the people of the Jews, concerning their restoration and their returning again into their own land' (in Silver, 1978, 188).

This belief that the messianic epoch was near at hand was based on several assumptions. First, the current tribulations of Israel were so intense that they could be nothing other than the sufferings prophesied in Scripture prior to the coming of the Messiah. 'Oh, how we have seen these things in the banishment of England, France and Spain!' (in Silver, 1978, 188), he wrote. The Inquisition, frequently involving martyrdoms, and universal persecution were the fulfilment of the prophet's warnings. Yet, he stated: 'if the Lord fulfil his words in calamities, he will fulfil it also in felicities' (in Silver, 1978, 189). A second factor was Israel's faithfulness during persecution. Such constancy illustrates that God has prepared a reward for the Israelite nation. Even now, he maintained, there is an indication of God's favour in the attainments of certain prominent Jews. A third conviction undergirding Manasseh's messianic beliefs was his view that Israel must be dispersed throughout the world before the Messiah can come. Such a view was based on Daniel 12:7: 'when the shattering of the power of the holy people comes to an end all these things would be accomplished'.

Finally, Manasseh stated that the prophecy of the two legs of the image of Nebuchadnezzer in Daniel 2, which will be overthrown by the fifth monarchy, refers to the

Ottoman Empire. As he wrote in his *Piedra Gloriosa o de la Estatua de Nebuchadnesar*:

> Whereby one sees in this prophecy five propositions diffusely expressed, namely:
>
> I. That by those four figures of beasts the four monarchies are signified, as it says in verse 17: these beasts are four, four monarchies, this being described with all the circumstances and typified by the statue of Nebuchadnesar.
>
> II. That the fourth monarchy will be divided into two nations, of different laws, this division being made by the little Mohammedan horn, and they are the two legs of the statue.
>
> III. That this Roman empire will be divided into ten king- doms, which are the ten horns derived from that beast and the ten toes of the statue.
>
> IV. That after the termination and destruction of these kingdoms there will follow the monarchy of Israel, as it is the holy people and the stone which turns into a mountain, filling up the whole world.
>
> V. That this monarchy of Israel will be temporal and terres- trial, as it says 'under the heaven', all that which the Lord revealeth to Nebuchadnesar, in a general way as to a heathen, he explained again with more diffusion and latitude and other circumstances perfectly to Daniel, revealing to him at the same time the duration of the fourth monarchy, although in such enigmatic terms that he alone understood them and kept them in his heart, as he affirms himself in the last words of this chapter. (in Silver, 1978, 190)

Responding to the Christian Paul Felgenhauer of Bohe- mia's contention that the coming of the Messiah was imminent, Manasseh stressed that a condition of the messianic age is Israel's supremacy over all nations. In a reply to Felgenhauer, he wrote:

> That good news brought by you, O most respected Sir, to the people of Israel in these recent times of affliction was the more welcome to my mind since, after the sorrows of so many ages and the long-deferring of our hopes, I have not ceased to desire the same most ardently ... So then, O worthy mes- senger of good things, is the arrival of our God at hand, who

pities us, and will he send in a short time to us the desire of so many ages, the Messiah at our head? ... As for what you say about the third sign of the coming of the Messiah, concerning this prediction of a kingdom of Israel throughout the world, that not only appears probable to me but we see something of the kind already coming to light and producing its effect. (in Silver, 1978, 166–7)

8

The Mystical Messiah

By the beginning of the seventeenth century Lurianic mysticism had made a major impact on Sephardi Jewry, and messianic expectations had become a central feature of Jewish life. In this milieu the arrival of a self-proclaimed messianic king, Shabbetai Tzevi brought about a transformation of Jewish life and thought. In 1665 his Messiahship was proclaimed by Nathan of Gaza; Shabbetai, he announced, would take the Sultan's crown, bring back the lost tribes and inaugurate the period of messianic redemption. In the following year Shabbetai journeyed to Constantinople, but on the order of the grand vizier he was arrested and put into prison. Within a short time the prison quarters became a messianic court – pilgrims from all over the world made their way to Constantinople to join in messianic rituals and ascetic activities. Eventually Shabbetai was brought to court and given the choice between conversion and death. In the face of this alternative, he converted to Islam and took on the name of Mehmed Effendi. Despite this act of apostasy, a number of his followers remained loyal justifying Shabbetai's action on the basis of kabbalistic ideas. After Shabbetai died in 1676, Nathan declared that he had ascended to the supernal world. In subsequent years such belief was continued by various branches of the Shabbatean movement. Other Jews, however, were deeply dispirited by Shabbetai's conversion: his failure to bring about messianic redemption was yet another chapter in the history of pseudo-Messiahs stretching back to the first century BCE.

Shabbetai Tzevi

In the history of Jewish messianism, the Shabbatean movement was the most dramatic messianic development since the destruction of the Second Temple in 70 CE. Born in Smyrna on the 9th of *Av* in 1626, Shabbetai was the son of Mordecai Tzevi who originated from the Peloponnesus and became a wealthy merchant. As a student of Isaac de Alba and Joseph Escapa, he received a traditional Jewish education, and appears to have been ordained as a *hakham* when he was about 18. According to one tradition, he left the *yeshivah* at the age of 15, embarking on a life of abstinence and solitude. In any event, he also commenced study of the *kabbalah*, concentrating on the *Zohar*, the *Sefer ha-Kanah* and *Sefer ha-Peliah*. After attaining a degree of expertise in kabbalistic study, he attracted a circle of young men to study with him.

From 1642 to 1648, Shabbetai lived a secluded life; during this time he experienced depression as well as euphoria – later these alternating moods were described by his followers as 'illumination' and 'fall'. During some of these periods of illumination, Shabbetai felt impelled to commit acts which violated Jewish law involving bizarre rituals and sudden innovations. Pre-eminent among these actions was the inclination to pronounce the Tetragrammaton (God's name). Conversely, during periods of melancholy, he retreated from human contact into solitude to wrestle with the demonic powers which assailed him.

It appears that when news of the Chmielnicki massacres reached Smyrna, Shabbetai uttered God's name in public and began to announce his Messiahship. Since Shabbetai's psychological states were well known, little attention was paid to such behaviour. Subsequently Shabbetai contracted two marriages in Smyrna; however since neither was consummated they ended in divorce. During this period Shabbetai related that a 'mystery of the Godhead' had been revealed to him, and he spoke of the 'God of faith' with whom he had a close relation. Of particular importance at this time was his use of the expression 'the God of Israel' which took on special mystical significance. Eventually his imagined acts of levitation and his repeated claims to be the Messiah led the rabbinic authorities to intervene, and he was banished from Smyrna.

In the years that followed Shabbetai wandered through Greece and Thrace, staying for some time with friends in Salonika. This sojourn, however, ended in disgrace since during one of his exalted states Shabbetai celebrated a nuptial service under the canopy of the Torah and committed other reprehensible acts. In 1658 he was expelled by the rabbis and travelled to Constantinople. There he became a friend of the celebrated kabbalist David Habillo. During this period Shabbetai attempted to rid himself of his demonic obsessions by means of kabbalistic practices. Nonetheless, during one of his ecstatic moods he celebrated the festivals of Passover, *Shavuot* and *Sukkot* in one week and proclaimed that the commandments should be abolished.

Expelled once again, he returned to Smyrna where he stayed until 1662; he then decided to travel to Jerusalem by way of Rhodes and Cairo. By the end of the year he arrived in Jerusalem, visiting the holy places and tombs of Jewish saints. In the autumn of 1663 he was sent as an emissary of the Jerusalem Jewish community. He then stayed in Cairo until 1665 and became closely involved with the circle around Raphael Joseph Chelebi, the head of Egyptian Jewry. Occasionally Shabbetai's messianic convictions returned, and it appears that during one of these occasions he resolved to marry an Ashkenazi Jewess of dubious reputation who had been an orphan of the 1648 Polish massacres and had gone first to Amsterdam, then Italy, and finally to Smyrna.

At this time news reached Shabbetai of a man of God who had appeared in Gaza possessed of miraculous powers. Convinced that this person, Nathan of Gaza, could provide him with a cure which would give peace to his soul, Shabbetai set out for Egypt. In 1665 he arrived in

Gaza; by this time Nathan had experienced a vision of Shabbetai as the Messiah – possibly this was the result of seeing Shabbetai in Jerusalem in 1663 and hearing tales about him from his teacher Jacob Hagiz under whom he had studied there. In any event, instead of relieving Shabbetai of his distress, Nathan sought to convince Shabbetai that he was the Messiah.

Initially Shabbetai refused to listen, but he nonetheless accompanied Nathan on his pilgrimages to some of the holy places in Jerusalem and Hebron. Eventually they returned to Gaza. According to one account, when they were celebrating *Shavuot*, Nathan fell into a trance and announced Shabbetai as the Messiah. Several days later Shabbetai had a further illumination of his messianic role, and on the 16th of *Sivan* he proclaimed himself as the Messiah. This was followed by several weeks of excitement. Riding on horseback, Shabbetai gathered together a group of followers and appointed them as his apostles.

In Palestine, news of Shabbetai's messiahship caused great frenzy even though it was opposed by a number of distinguished rabbis in Jerusalem. Despite such antagonism, Shabbetai circled the city several times on horseback, but was eventually banished from the town. Undeterred, Nathan declared that it was necessary for Jewry to repent and facilitate the coming redemption: as a consequence, excessive fasts and other forms of ascetic activity became prevalent, and letters were sent to Egypt and elsewhere announcing Shabbetai's wondrous deeds. Such news was accompanied by reports of the appearance of the Ten Lost Tribes of Israel.

In September 1665 Nathan wrote to Raphael Joseph, announcing that the time of redemption had come; in Nathan's view, Shabbetai would take the crown from the sultan and make him his servant. He would then proceed to the river Sambatyon and bring back the Lost Tribes and marry Rebecca, the daughter of Moses who will have been resurrected. During this time Shabbetai left Jerusalem and travelled to Aleppo where the Jewish masses were swept up in messianic frenzy. In Smyrna Shabbetai's ecstatic and bizarre activity divided the community. On 30 December Shabbetai sailed to Constantinople, convinced of his messianic mission.

On his arrival, however, he was arrested on the order of the grand vizier and put into prison. Within a short time the prison quarters became a messianic court; pilgrims from all over the world made their way to Constantinople to join in messianic rituals and ascetic activities. In addition, hymns were written in his honour and new festivals were introduced. According to Nathan, who remained in Gaza, the alteration in Shabbetai's moods from illumination to withdrawal symbolized his soul's struggle with demonic powers. At times he was imprisoned by the powers of evil (*kelippot*), but at other moments he prevailed against them.

During this period Shabbetai spent three days with the Polish kabbalist, Nehemiah ha-Kohen, who later denounced him to the Turkish authorities. Shabbetai was brought to court and given the choice between conversion and death. In the face of this alternative, he converted to Islam and took on the name of Aziz Mehmed Effendi. Such an act of apostasy scandalized most of his followers, but he defended himself by asserting that he had become a Muslim in obedience to God's commands. Many of his followers accepted this explanation and refused to give up their belief. Some thought it was not Shabbetai who had become a Muslim, but rather a phantom who had taken on his appearance; the Messiah himself had ascended to Heaven. Others cited biblical and rabbinic sources to justify Shabbetai's action.

Continuing to believe in Shabbetai, Nathan explained that the messianic task involved taking on the humiliation of being portrayed as a traitor to his people. Furthermore, he argued on the basis of Lurianic *kabbalah* that there were two kinds of divine light – a creative light and another light opposed to the existence of anything other than the *Ayn Sof* (Infinite). While creative light formed structures of creation in the empty space, the other light became after the *tzimtzum* (divine contraction) the power of evil. According to Nathan, the soul of the Messiah had been struggling against the power of evil from the beginning; his purpose was to allow divine light to penetrate this domain and bring about cosmic repair (*tikkun*). In order to do this, the soul of the Messiah was not obliged to keep the law, but was free to descend into the abyss to liberate the divine sparks and thereby conquer evil. In this light, Shabbetai's conversion to Islam was explicable.

After Shabbetai's act of apostasy, Nathan visited him in the Balkans and then travelled to Rome where he performed secret rites to bring about the end of the papacy. Shabbetai remained in Adrianople and Constantinople where he lived as both Muslim and Jew. In 1673 he was deported to Albania where he disclosed his own kabbalistic teaching to his supporters. After he died in 1676, Nathan declared that Shabbetai had ascended to the supernal world. Eventually a number of groups continued in their belief that Shabbetai was the Messiah, including a sect, the Dissidents (*Doenmeh*), which professed Islam publicly but nevertheless adhered to their own traditions.

The Shabbatean Movement

Shabbetai's conversion to Islam caused great consternation among his followers: many of his former disciples abandoned their belief in messianic redemption and left for their native lands. Nonetheless, not all of those who had accepted Shabbetai's messianic role deserted their leader, and Shabbatean groups flourished in Turkey, Italy and Poland where various figures claimed to be his legitimate successors. The biggest circles of Shabbateans in Turkey were located in Salonika, Smyrna and Constantinople.

In Constantinople the head of the Shabbateans was Abraham Yakhini who died in 1682. In Smyrna Abraham Cardozo played a leading role among the Shabbateans after he left Tripoli in 1673, and later Tunis and Leghorn – there he joined a large circle of followers of Shabbetai including the rabbi and preacher Elijah ben Solomon

Abraham ha-Kohen Ittamari and the cantor David Ben Israel Bonafoux. During this period Cardozo produced a wide range of literary works in which he expounded his interpretation of Shabbatean theology.

In his *Boker Abraham*, Cardozo argued that there is a difference between the God of the philosophers and the God of Israel who revealed himself to the Jewish people. In his view, the Jewish nation had been misled by the writings of such thinkers as Saadiah Gaon and Maimonides; only the teachers of the Talmud and the kabbalists have understood the true meaning of Torah. However, with the coming of messianic redemption, a few elect individuals will be able to penetrate the divine mysteries as conceived by Shabbetai. For some time Cardozo saw himself as the Messiah ben Joseph, the revealer of the true faith who must suffer before the advent of the Messiah ben David when all paradoxes of Shabbatean belief will be resolved. From 1680 to 1697 Cardozo lived in Constantinople, Rodosto and Adrianople where he aroused considerable consternation; eventually he lived in Candia, Chios and Egypt.

In Salonika, on the other hand, there existed a wide circle of believers in Shabbateanism including Shabbetai's last wife, her father Joseph Filosof, and her brother Jacob Querido as well as several important rabbis. After Nathan's death, visions of Shabbetai became increasingly common, leading to a mass conversion of about 300 families who became convinced they should follow Shabbetai's example. Along with those converts among Shabbetai's contemporaries, a new group led by Joseph Filosof and Solomon Florentin established a new sect, the *Doenmeh* who professed Islam in public but in private adhered to an heretical form of Judaism. Marrying among themselves, they were soon perceived as a distinct group by both Jews and Turks and developed into three sub-groups. Among these apostates, Baruchiah Russo created a further schism by teaching that the new messianic Torah called for a complete reversal of values, symbolized by an alteration of the 36 prohibitions of the Torah into positive obligations. It appears that this sect also developed the view that Shabbetai was divine; later Baruchiah was also seen as a divine figure.

Most of Shabbetai's followers, however, did not join the *Doenmeh* and remained within the Jewish fold. In Salonika, the Shabbateans eventually disappeared, but various rabbis such as Joseph ben David, Abraham Miranda, and Meir Bikayam were sympathetic to Shabbatean teaching. Those scholars who studied with Nathan and his pupils there – such as Solomon Ayllon and Elijah Mojajon – became rabbis of important Jewish communities and taught Shabbatean doctrine. During this period a significant number of emissaries from Palestine served as links between these believers in the diaspora.

Another centre of Shabbateanism existed in Italy, initially at Leghorn under Moses Pinheiro, Meir Rofe, Samuel de Paz and Judah Sharaf, and later in Modena. In Modena Abraham Rovigo was an exponent of a pietistic form of Shabbateanism and was frequently consulted by visitors to Italy from Israel, Poland and the Balkans. Such beliefs were shared by the rabbi of Reggio, Benjamin ben Eliezer ha-Kohen, as well as Hayyim Segré of Vercilli. In Modena revelations of heavenly *maggidim* who confirmed Shabbetai's role were common occurrences, and during this time a hagiography of Shabbetai was published by Baruch of Arezzo, one of Rovigo's group. Nathan's writings were also copied and studied, and figures who claimed heavenly inspiration (such as Isaachar Baer Perlhefter, Mordecai Eisenstadt from Prague, and Mordecai Ashkenazi from Zholkva) were supported by Rovigo. When Rovigo established a *yeshivah* in Jerusalem in 1701, most of its members were Shabbateans.

With the exception of the *Doenmeh*, most of Shabbetai's followers did not depart from the Jewish tradition. This was true of Ashkenazi Jewry as well. After Shabbetai's death, a number of Ashkenazi Shabbateans speculated that Shabbetai was the Messiah ben Joseph rather than the King-Messiah. Pre-eminent among those who adopted this position was Mordecai Eisenstadt; together with his brother he travelled through Bohemia, southern Germany and northern Italy encouraging the masses not to lose faith in messianic redemption. During this period, various claimants for the role of Messiah ben Joseph also came forward, such as Joseph ibn Zur in Meknès who proclaimed that the final redemption would take place at Passover in 1675. Another messianic pretender was the silversmith Joshua Heshel ben Joseph who became the leading spokesman of the Shabbatean movement in Poland. His *Sefer ha-Zoref*, based on mystical and numerological explanations of *Shema Yisrael*, alleged that he was the Messiah ben Joseph, and Shabbetai was the Messiah ben David. Another prophet of this period was a brandy distiller named Zadok who appeared in 1694 to 1696 in Gradno.

These messianic figures had an enormous impact on Jewry as far away as Italy, where Rovigo and his associates collected testimonies from various Polish visitors such as Hayyim ben Solomon from Kalisz (Hayyim Malakh). In 1691 he came to Italy to study the writings of Nathan which had not become available in Poland; after his return he disseminated Nathan's ideas among the rabbis of Poland. Subsequently he went to Adrianople, and became a spokesman for the more radical branch of the Shabbatean movement, joining forces with Judah Hasid from Shidlov – from 1696 to 1700 they became the leaders of the 'holy society of Rabbi Judah Hasid', a group consisting of hundreds of Shabbateans who engaged in extreme asceticism and planned to emigrate to Palestine to wait for Shabbetai's second coming. Groups of these individuals travelled through Polish and German communities spreading Shabbatean doctrine. By the end of 1698, a council of Shabbatean leaders was held in Mikulov.

The emigration of Shabbateans to Jerusalem in 1700 signified the high point of Shabbatean activity. However, the movement suffered great disappointment in its earliest stages. Judah Hasid died on his arrival in October 1700, and dissension erupted between moderates and the more radical elements led by Malakh who were expelled.

Yet even the moderates were not able to settle in the Holy Land, and many returned to Germany, Austria and Poland. Many believers had expected Shabbetai's return in 1706; when this did not materialize, the movement was further weakened and driven underground. As time passed, the Shabbateans were identified with the extremist antinomian wing of the movement. Malakh went to Salonika, and then spread his radical antinomian interpretation of Shabbateanism in Podolia.

In time Shabbateanism divided into two different factions. The moderates provided literary works which reached a wide public which was unaware of the messianic convictions of their authors. The radicals, on the other hand, became increasingly active after Baruchiah had been proclaimed 'Santo Señor' and an incarnation of the Shabbatean interpretation of the 'God of Israel'. Through emissaries from Salonika and Podolia, they circulated manuscripts and letters expounding their kabbalistic views. The circles of Hasidim in Poland prior to the emergence of the Baal Shem Tov were deeply influenced by Shabbatean doctrine. In Moravia Judah ben Jacob (Loebele Prossnitz) caused considerable turmoil after his awakening as a Shabbatean prophet. Travelling through Moravia and Silesia, he attracted a wide circle of followers even after his magical practices were exposed and he was put under a ban – Prossnitz remained as the headquarters of a sizable Shabbatean group throughout the century. Subsequently another centre of Shabbateanism arose in Mannheim where members of Judah Hasid's society found refuge.

While these events were taking place, a major scandal erupted when Nehemiah Hiyya Hayon from Sarajevo published a work of Shabbatean theology. Compelled to leave the Holy Land because of his Shabbatean activities, he lived for some years in Turkey, and eventually settled in Venice where he published three books dealing with Shabbatean theory. In 1713 he went to Amsterdam where he lived under the protection of Solomon Ayllon who was a secret adherent of Shabbateanism. During this time a violent debate took place between the rabbis of the Amsterdam Sephardi and Ashkenazi rabbis where Shab-batean theology was discussed publicly. In this controversy Hayon defended his kabbalistic doctrine, but denied its Shabbatean character. By the end of 1715 Hayon was compelled to leave Europe, but he returned in 1725 when a further Shabbatean scandal erupted.

This controversy was connected with increasing propa-ganda of the followers of Baruchiah who were established in Podolia, Moravia, and particularly in the *yeshivah* of Prague where Jonathan Eybeschuetz was an active sup-porter. From 1724 various kabbalistic tracts were circu-lated from Prague, and Eybeschuetz was widely believed to be their author. When various Shabbatean writings from Baruchiah's sect were discovered in Frankfurt in 1725 among the luggage of Moses Meir of Kamenka, a network of Shabbatean propagandists was revealed. Because of Eybeschuetz's reputation as an eminent talmudist, no action was taken against him, especially since he became the leader of those who publicly condemned Shabbetai Tzvei and his followers. In other communities in Poland, Germany and Austria, similar declarations were pub-lished, demanding that the secret Shabbateans should be denounced to the rabbinical authorities.

However, it was later revealed that Eybeschuetz had given out a number of amulets in Metz and Hamburg of a Shabbatean character: this caused a further controversy. His main opponent, Jacob Emden, accused him of Shab-batean tendencies; in response Eybeschuetz argued that the text of these amulets consisted only of mystical Holy Names that were part of the kabbalistic tradition. In central Europe, Eybeschuetz was regarded by secret Shab-bateans as an advocate of their theological doctrine; the orthodox, however, were outraged that a leading rabbinic authority could embrace such heretical notions.

During this period controversy also erupted about the revelations of Moses Hayyim Luzzatto in Padua. Although in his writings Luzzatto repudiated the claims of Shab-betai Zevi, he appears to have been influenced by

Shabbatean teaching, particularly concerning the prehistory of the Messiah's soul in the realm of the *kelippot*. Even though the heretical aspects of these ideas were eliminated, Luzzatto sought to find a place for Shabbetai in his theology. Another debate about Shabbatean doctrine centred on the publication of an anonymous work which described in detail Jewish life and ritual from the standpoint of Lurianic *kabbalah*. This work was permeated by ascetic Shabbateanism, and included several hymns written by Nathan of Gaza as well as a ritual for the evening of the new moon with Shabbatean connotations. After its publication in 1742, it was denounced by Jacob Emden.

Frankists

The Frankist movement was the last stage in the development of Shabbateanism. Born in Korolowka, Podolia, Jacob Frank was educated in Czernowitz and Sniatyn, living for several years in Bucharest where he worked as a dealer in cloth and precious stones. It appears that Frank associated at an early stage with the Shabbateans connected with the radical wing of the movement. Accompanied by these teachers, he visited Salonika in 1753 and became involved with the Baruchiah group of the *Doenmeh*. Later he journeyed to the grave of Nathan of Gaza as well as Adrianople and Smyrna. Eventually he emerged as the leader of the Shabbateans in Poland where he was perceived by his followers as a reincarnation of the divine soul which had previously resided in Shabbetai and Baruchiah.

In 1755 Frank, accompanied by R. Mordecai and R. Nahman, spent time with his relatives in Korolewka; he then journeyed through the communities in Podolia which contained Shabbatean groups. Although he was received enthusiastically by Shabbateans, his appearance in Lanskroun caused considerable consternation when he was discovered conducting a Shabbatean ritual with his followers; his opponents claimed that a religious orgy was taking place similar to the rites practised by members of the Baruchiah sect in Podolia. Although Frank's followers were imprisoned, he was released because the authorities thought he was a Turkish subject. At the request of the local rabbis an enquiry was instituted in Satanow which examined the practices of the Shabbateans.

Frank then crossed the Turkish frontier and was arrested in March 1756 but again allowed to go free. Subsequently he remained in Turkey where he became a convert to Islam. In June and August 1757 Frank made secret visits to Podolia to confer with his followers. When Frank appeared in Poland, he was regarded as the central figure for the Shabbatean community. The rabbinic authorities, however, were deeply troubled by the findings of the Satanow inquiry: it became clear that the Shabbateans transgressed various Jewish laws including sexual prohibitions of the Torah. The results of this examination were presented to a rabbinical assembly at Brody and confirmed at a session of the Council of the Four Lands held in Konstantynow. In Brody a *herem* (excommunication) was issued against the members of the sect which led to widespread persecution of the Shabbateans particularly in Podolia. To protect themselves from such antagonism Frank's followers put themselves under the protection of Bishop Dembowski of Kamieniec-Podolski in whose diocese many of them lived. On Frank's advice, they stressed the beliefs they held in common with Christians; in addition, they issued anti-Jewish propaganda at the instigation of their Christian protectors.

After the Brody *herem* was issued, the Frankists asked Bishop Dembowski to hold a new enquiry into the affair that took place at Lanskroun and petitioned that a disputation be arranged between themselves and the rabbis. In June 1757 a confrontation took place at Kamieniec involving nineteen opponents of the Talmud with several rabbis from local communities. Later in the year Bishop Dembowski issued his decision in favour of the Frankists and imposed a series of penalties on the rabbis including a decree that the Talmud be burned. However, after the Bishop's death, the Frankists were persecuted by the

Jewish community, causing many to flee to Turkey where they converted to Islam. Other Frankists turned to the political and ecclesiastic authorities for permission to follow their own faith. In June 1758 King Augustus III granted the sectarians royal protection, and many refugees returned to Podolia. In January 1759 Frank also returned from Turkey and settled in Iwanie where he revealed himself as the living embodiment of God's power who had arrived to fulfil the mission of Shabbetai and Baruchiah. Rejecting traditional Shabbatean theology, he propounded a new system in which it was necessary for believers to adopt the Christian faith. In his view, Jesus was a husk preceding and concealing the true fruit which was Frank himself as the true Messiah. Continuing the tradition of Baruchiah's sect, Frank instituted licentious sexual practices among the believers.

As time passed, it became clear that Frank and his followers would need to be baptized and they requested that Archbishop Lubieński in Lvov receive them into the Church. In making this application, they expressed the wish to be allowed to lead a separate existence. The Church, however, replied that no special privileges would be granted. In July 1759 a disputation took place in Lvov as a precondition to conversion; there leading rabbis and members of the Frankist sect debated a variety of theological topics as well as the blood libel charge. In September 1759 Frank himself was baptized, and by the end of 1760 in Lvov alone more than 500 Frankists followed his example.

Despite such widespread conversion, the Church became increasingly suspicious of the Frankists: it appeared that the real object of their devotion was Frank as the living incarnation of God. In February 1760 Frank was arrested and an inquisition took place; this resulted in Frank's exile to the fortress of Czestochowa. Despite his absence, his followers organized themselves into a network of secret sects. From the end of 1760 Frank's disciples began to visit him; in time the conditions of Frank's imprisonment were relaxed and from 1762 his wife was permitted to join him and a group of followers were allowed to settle near the fortress.

In 1765 Frank planned to establish links with the Russian Orthodox Church and the Russian government. At the end of the year a Frankist delegation went to Smolensk and Moscow. Two years later a counterdelegation was sent to St Petersburg to inform the Russians of Frank's true nature. In response Frankist propaganda spread throughout the communities of Galicia, Hungary, Moravia and Bohemia, and links were formed with Shabbateans in Germany. When Czestochowa was captured by the Russians in August 1772, Frank was freed and went to Warsaw and later to Bruenn in Moravia.

Remaining in Bruenn, Frank gained the protection of the authorities since he pledged to work for the spread of Christianity among his followers in Moravia. In March 1775 Frank and his daughter went to Vienna where they were received by the empress and her son. During this period Frank predicted that a revolution would take place that would overthrow the kingdoms of the earth and dreamed of the conquest of a territory that would be reserved for the Frankist community. While in Bruenn, his teachings were taken down by his chief associates. Eventually Frank moved to Offenbach, near Frankfurt. In both Bruenn and Offenbach, Frank and his children pretended to live as Catholics while adopting various strange oriental practices; at this time Frank also spread the rumour that his daughter Eva was the illegitimate daughter of Catherine of the house of Romanov. In December 1791 Frank died, mourned by hundreds of his followers.

During the period between Frank's apostasy and his death, a number of members of the movement gained great wealth, particularly in Warsaw where they built factories and were involved in masonic activities. A group of about 50 families settled in Bukovina after his death and became known as the Abrahmites. Other families in Moravia and Bohemia maintained close connections with the *Haskalah*, combining kabbalistic notions with the rationalistic outlook of the Enlightenment. Only occasionally did entire groups of Frankists convert to Christianity, but a large number of younger members who were sent to Offenbach were baptized.

After Frank's death it appears that Franz Thomas von Schoenfeld was offered the leadership of the sect; when he refused, Eva together with her younger brothers, Josef and Rochus assumed control of the court. Many continued to travel to Offenbach, however Frank's daughters and brothers did not have the force of personality to exercise leadership of the movement. By 1803 Offenbach was nearly deserted and Frank's children were reduced to poverty. In the first decade of the nineteenth century Josef and Rochus died, and Eva died in 1816. Despite this demise the sect's organization continued to survive through emissaries, secret gatherings, and the dissemination of Frankist literature, and members of the sect endeavoured to marry only among themselves. In Germany, Bohemia and Moravia Frankists usually held summer gatherings in Carlsbad at about the time of *Tisha B'Av*.

The literary output of the Frankists began at the end of Frank's life; centred at Offenbach, three elders – Franciszek and Michael Wolowski and Andreas Dembowski – compiled a collection of Frank's sayings which was distributed among believers. In addition, a detailed chronicle of Frank's life was compiled. Prague was another centre of literary activity: there Jonas Wehle and his brothers and son-in-law wrote down many of the teachings of the movement. Despite the attacks made on the Frankists by rabbinic authorities, a small group survived.

On Eva Frank's death, the organization diminished in strength even though Elias Kaplinski – a member of Frank's wife's family – summoned a conference of sectarians in Carlsbad. After this event, the sect disbanded and emissaries were sent to collect together the various writings of the movement. In 1848–9 a group of Frankists from Bohemia and Moravia migrated to the United States. Despite such disintegration, there still remained a number of Frankist families who continued to marry only among themselves, and for some time this circle maintained secret contacts with the *Doenmeh* in Salonika.

Early Hasidism

By the middle of the eighteenth century, the Jewish community had suffered numerous waves of persecution and was deeply dispirited by the conversion of Shabbetai Tzevi as well as the growth of Shabbateanism. In this environment the Hasidic movement – grounded in *kabbalah* – sought to revitalize Jewish life. The founder of this new movement was Israel ben Eliezer known as the Baal Shem Tov (or Besht). According to tradition, Israel ben Eleazar was born in southern Poland and in his twenties journeyed with his wife to the Carpathian mountains. In the 1730s he travelled to Mezibozh where he performed various miracles and instructed his disciples in kabbalistic lore. By the 1740s he had attracted a considerable number of disciples who passed on his teaching.

Rejecting the asceticisim of the *kabbalah*, the Besht emphasized the importance of joy in worship. 'Our Father in Heaven,' he stated, 'hates sadness and rejoices when his children are joyful. And when are his children joyful? When they carry out his commandments.' For the Besht worshipping with spontaneity is the keynote to the religious life: thus he stressed that enthusiasm and ecstasy should replace formalism in prayer. According to the Besht, in each Jew there is a spark of holiness which needs to be kindled. In his view, evil does not exist. Thus once he was asked by a distraught father: 'What shall I do with my son, he is so wicked?' The Besht replied: 'Love him all the more.' Wherever he went, the Besht sought to bring back the wayward of Israel. In this quest, the Besht was anxious to draw Jews back to the tradition through mercy and compassion.

The Besht maintained that he had come into the world to show human beings how to live by three precepts: love of God, love of Israel, and love of the Torah. In a letter to

his brother-in-law, he declared that this mission was part
of God's providential plan as was revealed to him by the
Messiah in a heavenly ascent:

> I went higher step by step until I entered the palace of the
> Messiah wherein the Messiah studies the Torah together with
> all the *tannaim* and the saints and also with the Seven
> Shepherds. There I witnessed great rejoicing and could not
> fathom the reason for it so I thought that, God forbid, the
> rejoicing was over my own departure from the world. But I
> was afterwards informed that I was not yet to die since they
> took great delight on high when, through their Torah, I
> perform unifications here below. (in Cohn-Sherbok, 1994,
> 63)

On this ascent the Besht confronted the Messiah and
asked him when he would come. In reply the Messiah
declared that it will occur when the Besht's teaching is
revealed to the world and others will be able to perform
unifications and have ascents of the soul. Then, he stated,
all the *kellipot* will be consumed and it will be a time of
grace and salvation.

The hope for messianic redemption was thus a central
feature of early Hasidism, yet the movement called for a
reorientation of Jewish life. After the death of the Baal
Shem Tov, Dov Baer of Mezhirich became the leader of
this sect and Hasidism spread to southern Poland, the
Ukraine and Lithuania. The growth of this movement
engendered considerable hostility on the part of rabbinic
authorities. In particular the rabbinic leadership of Vilna
issued an edict of excommunication; the Hasidim were
charged with permissiveness in their observance of the
commandments, laxity in the study of the Torah, excess in
prayer, and preference for the Lurianic rather than the
Ashkenazic prayerbook. In subsequent years the Hasidim
and their opponents (the *Mitnagdim*) bitterly denounced
one another.

Relations deteriorated further when Jacob Joseph of
Polonnoye published a book critical of the rabbinate: his
work was burned and in 1781 the *Mitnagdim* ordered that
all relations with the Hasidim cease. By the end of the

century the Jewish religious establishment of Vilna denounced the Hasidim to the Russian government, an act which resulted in the imprisonment of several leaders. Despite such condemnation the Hasidic movement was eventually recognized by the Russian and Austrian governments; in the ensuing years the movement divided into a number of separate groups under different leaders who passed on positions of authority to their descendants.

Hasidism initiated a profound change in Jewish religious pietism. In the medieval period, the *Hasidei Ashkenaz* attempted to achieve perfection through various mystical activities. This tradition was carried on by Lurianic kabbalists who engaged in various forms of self-mortification. In opposition to such ascetic practices, the Besht and his followers emphasized the omnipresence of God rather than the shattering of the vessels and the imprisonment of divine sparks by the powers of evil. Here there was a conscious attempt to distance the movement from the Shabbateans who believed that such a liberation of imprisoned sparks was carried out by Shabbetai Tzevi. For Hasidic Judaism there is no place where God is absent; the doctrine of the *tzimtzum* (divine contraction) was interpreted by sages as only an apparent withdrawal of the divine presence. Divine light, they believed, is everywhere.

For some Hasidim cleaving to God (*devekut*) in prayer was understood as the annihilation of selfhood and the ascent of the soul to divine light. In this context, joy, humility, gratitude and spontaneity were seen as essential features of Hasidic worship. The central obstacles to concentration in prayer are distracting thoughts; according to Hasidism such sinful intentions contain a divine spark which can be released. In this regard the traditional kabbalistic stress on theological speculation was replaced by a preoccupation with mystical psychology in which inner bliss was conceived as the highest aim rather than repair (*tikkun*) of the cosmos. For the Beshtian Hasidim it was also possible to achieve *devekut* in daily activities including eating, drinking, business affairs and sex. Such ordinary acts become religious if in performing them one cleaves to God, and *devekut* is thus attainable by all Jews rather than a scholarly elite. Unlike the earlier mystical tradition, Hasidism provided a means by which ordinary Jews could reach a state of spiritual ecstasy. Hasidic worship embraced singing, dancing and joyful devotion in anticipation of the period of messianic redemption.

Another central feature of this new movement was the institution of the *zaddik* (or *rebbe*) which gave expression to a widespread disillusionment with rabbinic leadership. According to Hasidism, the *zaddikim* are spiritually superior individuals who have attained the highest level of *devekut*. The goal of the *zaddik* is to elevate the souls of his flock to the divine light; his tasks include pleading to God for his people, immersing himself in their everyday affairs, and counselling and strengthening them. As an authoritarian figure the *zaddik* was seen by his followers as possessing miraculous power to ascend to the divine realm.

In this context *devekut* to God involved cleaving to the *zaddik*. Given this emphasis on the role of the *rebbe*, Hasidic literature including summaries of the spiritual and kabbalistic teachings of various famous *zaddikim* as well as stories about their miraculous deeds. Foremost among these leading figures was Zusya of Hanipol, Shneur Zalman of Liady, Levi Yitzhak of Berdichev and Nahman of Bratzlav. These various leaders developed their own customs, doctrines and music and gathered around themselves disciples who made pilgrimages to their courts in the Ukraine and in Polish Galicia. In central Poland Hasidism emphasized the centrality of faith and Talmudic study; Lubavich Hasidim in Lithuania, on the other hand, combined kabbalistic speculation and rabbinic scholarship. Yet despite the movement's break from traditional patterns of Jewish life, Hasidism continued to await the coming of the Messiah who would fulfil all Scriptural prophecies and usher in a period of deliverance and redemption.

9

Messianic and Anti-Messianic Zionism

With the conversion of Shabbetai Tzevi in the seventeenth century, the Jewish preoccupation with messianic calculation diminished. Nonetheless, there emerged a number of religious Zionists who continued to subscribe to the belief in the advent of the messianic era. Prominent among such figures was Yehudai hai Alkalai, who maintained that Jewish settlers should establish Jewish colonies in Palestine in anticipation of the coming of the Messiah. A similar view was adopted by Zwi Hirsch Kalischer, who argued that the messianic era will not take place immediately; rather, the redemption of the Jewish people will occur gradually through the ingathering of the Jewish nation in their ancient homeland. Later Abraham Isaac Kook sought to harmonize messianic aspirations with the efforts of modern secular Zionists. Opposed to this reinterpretation of messianic deliverance, Orthodox critics of Zionism united in their opposition to what they perceived as a betrayal of traditional Jewish values. In their view, it is forbidden to accelerate divine redemption through human efforts. Distancing themselves from traditional belief in messianic redemption, other Jews adopted a secular approach to Jewish nationalism. In the view of such figures as Moses Hess, Leon Pinsker and Theodor Herzl, the creation of a Jewish homeland is required to solve the problem of anti-Semitism. Only by establishing their own nation will Jews be able to protect themselves from anti-Jewish assault. Rejecting the Zionist cause, liberal Jews attacked both messianic and secular Zionism for its utopian character. According to these reformers, what is now required is for Jews to accommodate themselves to the cultures in which they live and achieve security through a policy of assimilation.

Religious Zionism

In the nineteenth century within Orthodoxy there emerged a new development, the advocacy of an active approach to Jewish Messianism. Rather than passively await the coming of the Messiah, these writers argued that the Jewish people must engage in the creation of a homeland in anticipation of divine redemption. Pre-eminent among such religious Zionists was Yehuda hai Alkalai, born in 1798 in Sarajevo to Rabbi Sholomo Alkalai, the spiritual leader of the local Jewish community. During his youth he lived in Palestine where he was influenced by kabbalistic thought. In 1825 he served as a rabbi in Semlin in Serbia, and in 1834 he published a booklet entitled *Shema Yisrael* in which he advocated the establishment of Jewish colonies in Palestine. When in 1840 the Jews of Damascus were charged with the blood libel, he became convinced that the Jewish nation could be secure only in their own land. As a result, he published a series of books and pamphlets explaining his plan of self-redemption.

In his *Minhat Yehuda* he argued on the basis of the Bible that the Messiah will not miraculously materialize; rather he will be preceded by a chain of preparatory events. In this light the Holy Land needs to be populated by Jewry in preparation for messianic deliverance. For Alkalai, redemption is not simply a divine affair – it is also a human concern requiring labour and persistence. He writes:

> This new redemption will be different; our land is waste and desolate, and we shall have to build houses, dig wells, and plant vines and olive trees. We are, therefore, commanded not to attempt to go at once and all together into the Holy Land. (in Hertzberg, 1969, 105)

This demystification of traditional messianic eschatology extends to Alkalai's advocacy of Hebrew as the national language. Traditionally Hebrew was viewed as a sacred language reserved for religious use. Alkalai, however, stressed the practical importance of having a single language for ordinary life in Palestine:

> I wish to attest to the pain I have always felt at the error of our ancestors, that they allowed our Holy Tongue to be so forgotten. Because of this our people was divided into seventy peoples; our one language was replaced by the seventy languages of the lands of exile. If the Almighty should indeed show us his miraculous favour and gather us into our land, we would not be able to speak to each other and such a divided community could not succeed. (in Hertzberg, 1969, 106)

In Alkalai's view the Jewish people must now ensure that Hebrew is studied so that it can be used for ordinary life.

To accomplish the process of redemption, Alkalai emphasized the importance of gathering together an assembly of those dedicated to the realization of this goal. Hence he contended that the redemption must begin with efforts by Jews themselves. Reinterpreting the concept of the Messiah ben Joseph, he argued that this assembly of elders is in fact what is meant by the promise of the Messiah, the son of Joseph. For Alkalai, the process of deliverance follows a different sequence from what is outlined in traditional sources. The vision of this first messianic figure should be understood as a process involving the emergence of a political leadership among the Jewish nation that would prepare the way for redemption.

Another early pioneer of religious Zionism was Zwi Hirsch Kalischer, the rabbi of Toun. An early defender of Orthodoxy against Reform Judaism, he championed the commandments prescribing faith in the Messiah and devotion to the Holy Land. In 1836 he expressed his commitment to Jewish settlement in Palestine in a letter to the Rothschilds: 'The beginning of the redemption will come through natural causes by human effort and by the will of the governments to gather the scattered of Israel into the Holy Land' (in Hertzberg, 1969, 109–10).

Such a belief did not actively engage Kalischer until 1860 when a society was organized in Frankfurt on the Oder to encourage Jewish settlement in Palestine. After joining this group, he published *Derishat Zion*. In this work he advocated the return of Jewry to its native soil. The redemption of Israel, he argued, will not take place miraculously:

> The Almighty, blessed be his Name, will not suddenly descend from on high and command his people to go forth. Neither will he send the Messiah from heaven in a twinkling of an eye, to sound the great trumpet for the scattered of Israel and gather them into Jerusalem. He will not surround the holy city with a wall of fire or cause the holy Temple to descend from heaven. (Avineri, 1981, 53)

Rather, the redemption will take place slowly, through awakening support from philanthropists and gaining the agreement of other nations to the ingathering of the Jewish people into its ancestral home.

The coming of the Messiah must thus be preceded by the creation of a Jewish homeland. It is not enough to wait for miracles; rather Jews should act to hasten this event. Practical steps must therefore be taken to fulfil this dream of resettlement. What is required is an organization to encourage emigration and purchase and cultivate farms and vineyards. This programme would be a ray of deliverance to those who now languish in Palestine due to poverty and famine – this situation would be totally changed if those able to contribute to this effort were inspired by the vision of a Jewish homeland. One advantage of this scheme would be to bring to fruition those religious commandments that are attached to working the soil in the Holy Land. Even those Jews who supervised the labourers would be aiding in the working of the land and would therefore have the same status as if they had personally fulfilled these commandments. Yet beyond all this, Kalischer was persuaded that Jewish farming would be a spur to messianic redemption. By working the land, Jews would be dedicating themselves to bringing about the advent of the Messianic Age.

Following in the footsteps of such religious Zionists as Alkalai and Kalischer, Abraham Isaac Kook formulated a vision of messianic redemption integrating the creation of a Jewish state. Born in Greiva, Latvia in 1865, Kook received a traditional Jewish education, and in 1895 became rabbi of Bausk. In 1904 he emigrated to Palestine where he served as a rabbi of Jaffa. Eventually he was elected Ashekazi head of the new court of appeals (in effect the Ashkenazi chief rabbi of Palestine), and served in this post until his death in 1935.

Unlike secularists who advocated practical efforts to secure a Jewish state, Kook embarked on the task of reinterpreting the Jewish religious tradition to transform religious messianic longing into the basis for collaboration with the aspirations of modern Zionism. According to Kook, the centrality of Israel is a fundamental feature of Jewish life and a crucial element of Jewish consciousness. Nonetheless, the fervent belief in messianic deliverance has not been accompanied by an active policy of resettlement. This distinction between religious aspirations for the return from exile and the desire of many Jews to live in the diaspora highlights the confusion in Jewish thinking about the role of Israel in Jewish life. There is thus a contradiction between the messianic belief in a return to Zion and the accommodating attitude to exile of most Jews throughout history.

For Kook, the attachment to the land of Israel must serve as the foundation of Jewish life in the modern world. Although the secular pioneers who came to Palestine were motivated by ideological convictions alien to traditional Judaism, their actions are paradoxically part of God's plan of redemption. In the cosmic scheme of the divine will, seemingly atheistic and secular actions are absorbed into the unfolding of God's plan. Therefore, these pioneers unintentionally contributed to the coming of the Messiah

– without consciously acknowledging the significance of their work, they served God's purpose.

Such observations led Kook to insist that the divine spark is manifest in the work of secular Zionists who sacrificed themselves for the land of Israel. Such pioneers were not godless blasphemers, but servants of the Lord. Unaware of their divine mission, they actively engaged in bringing about God's Kingdom on earth. This redemptive vision of a global transformation of human life is directly related to the aspiration of earlier Jewish writers who awaited the return of the Messiah to bring about the end of human history. For Kook, on the other hand, the rebuilding of a Jewish state, even by secular, atheistic pioneers, is an essential ingredient for this process of universal salvation and divine redemption.

Orthodox Anti-Zionism

Even though some Orthodox figures endorsed Zionism, the majority of Orthodox Jews in Germany, Hungary and Eastern European countries protested against this new development in Jewish life. To advance this policy an ultra-Orthodox group, *Agudat Israel*, was formed in 1912 to unite rabbis and laity against the Zionist movement. Although the Torah maintains that it is the duty of religious Jews to return to the Holy Land, these Orthodox critics emphasized that such an ingathering of the exiles must be preceded by messianic redemption. Before the rise of Zionism, the nineteenth-century scholar and leader of German Jewish Orthodoxy, Samson Raphael Hirsch, argued that it is forbidden actively to accelerate divine deliverance. In the light of such teaching, Zionism was perceived by the strictly Orthodox as a conspiracy against God's will and equated with pseudo-messianism. Pre-eminent among such Orthodox figures was Zadok of Lublin who stated that he prayed to the Lord for the day of redemption, but was unwilling to settle in Palestine out of fear that such an act could be interpreted as condoning the Zionist movement.

Despite such views, Scripture decrees that it is obligatory for Jews to return to Zion, and this prescription called
for an Orthodox response. Accordingly, ultra-Orthodox
figures differentiated between the duty to return to the
Holy Land and the duty of residing there. Strictly observ-
ant Jews, they maintained, were exempt from actually
settling in the land because of such factors as physical
danger, economic difficulties, inability to educate the
young, and so forth. Further, these critics stressed that
Zionism was not simply a movement to rebuild Palestine;
it was also an heretical attempt to usurp the privilege of
the Messiah to establish a Jewish kingdom.

In addition, ultra-Orthodox spokesmen declared that
Zionism sought to leave religion out of the national life; as
a consequence, the Jewish state would betray the ideals of
the Jewish heritage. Throughout its history, the nation
had been animated by spiritual ideals, and refused to
perish because of its adherence to traditional precepts. If
Israel endured through thousands of years of persecution,
then it would be folly to abandon the religious values
which kept alive the hope for Jewish survival. Thus,
ideologists of the ultra-right such as Isaac Breuer insisted
that Zionism was depriving the Jewish nation of its commitment in a misguided pursuit of modern conceptions of
nationhood. This, he contended, was the most pernicious
form of assimilation.

For these reasons *Agudat Israel* condemned the policies
of modern Zionists and refused to collaborate with religious parties such as the *Mizrahi*. In Palestine itself ultra-
Orthodox Jews joined with *Agudat Israel* in its struggle
against Zionism. Frequently its leaders protested to the
British government and the League of Nations about the
Zionist quest to create a national home in Palestine.
Occasionally it even joined forces with Arab leaders. This
conflict eventually led to the murder of a member of the
executive of the *Agudat,* Jacob Israel de Han. A Dutch Jew
by origin, de Han denounced Zionism in cables to British
newspapers, attacking the Balfour Commission and British officers for their seemingly pro-Zionist stance. On 30

June 1924 he was assassinated in Jerusalem by the Haga-
nah without knowledge of the high command. For the
ultra-Orthodox Jews of Jerusalem, de Han became a
martyr for the glory of God: this incident illustrated the
depths of hatred of Zionism among right-wing Orthodox
Jews. According to the ultra-Orthodox spokesman Joseph
Sonnenfeld, Zionists were evil men and ruffians; Hell, he
believed, had entered Israel with Herzl.

Despite this initial attack on the Zionist enterprise,
these critics of Zionist aspirations modified their position
and began to take a more active role in Jewish settlement.
This was due to the immigration of members of *Agudat
Israel* to Palestine, as well as the massacre of Orthodox
Jews in Hebron, Safed and Jerusalem during the Arab
riots of 1929. Nonetheless, the ultra-right refused to join
the National Council of Palestinian Jewry which had been
created in the 1920s. In the next decades the rise of the
Nazis and the events of the Holocaust brought about a
split in the movement.

In 1934 Isaac Breuer declared: 'Do not leave Jewish
history to the Zionists.' If *Agudat* wished to gain the upper
hand against the Zionists, it was obliged to prepare the
Holy Land for the rule of God. In the unfolding of God's
providential plan for his chosen people, the extreme
Orthodox had a crucial role to play. Four years later
Breuer asked the General Assembly of the *Agudat* to
decide whether the Balfour Declaration was part of God's
providential scheme or satanic in origin. Although some
Orthodox leaders in Palestine were sympathetic to Breuer's
views, other prominent members remained unconvinced.
Such figures as Jacob Rosenheim, the political head of
Central European Orthodoxy, maintained that even after
the Holocaust the Zionist quest to evacuate Europe and
gather up the exiles was a mistake since it is impossible to
ascertain what God had planned for his chosen people
prior to the arrival of the Messiah.

Between the end of the War and the founding of the
Jewish State a zealous extreme group, the *Neturei Karta*
('Guardians of the City') in Jerusalem accused the *Agudat*

of succumbing to the Zionist cause. Headed by Amram
Blau and Aharon Katzenellenbogen, these extremists
were supported by the followers of rabbis in Brisk
(Poland) and Szatmar (Hungary) who had emigrated to
the United States and other Western countries. According
to the *Neturei Karta*, those who accepted the Jewish State
were apostates, and the rabbis who supported *Agudat* were
seen as leading the new generation away from Torah
Judaism. As a result of these policies, these zealots refused
to participate in the Israeli War of Independence,
demanded an internationalization of Jerusalem under the
supervision of the United Nations, rejected Israeli identity
cards, and were unwilling to acknowledge Israel as a State.
Yet despite such an uncompromising position, the leaders
of *Agudat Israel* continued to support the creation of a
Jewish homeland and a year before its establishment they
reached an understanding with Palestinian Zionists concerning such matters as Sabbath observance, dietary laws,
and regulations concerning education and marriage.
Such a conciliatory stance paved the way for *Agudat*'s
participation in Israeli political life and its membership in
the United Religious Front.

Secular Zionism

Unlike such figures as Alkalai, Kalischer and Kook, modern secular Zionists have been preoccupied with the
problem of anti-Semitism rather than messianic deliverance. The nineteenth-century writer Moses Hess, for
example, argued that anti-Jewish sentiment is inevitable;
no reform of Judaism is able to eliminate Jew-hatred from
Western society. Born in Bonn, Germany, Hess published
his first philosophical work in 1837; by 1840 he had settled
in Paris where he was active in socialist circles. Several
decades later he published *Rome and Jerusalem*, a systematic defence of Jewish nationalism.

In this work Hess argued that anti-Jewish sentiment is
unavoidable. Progressive Jews believe they can escape
from Judeophobia by recoiling from any Jewish national

expression, yet the hatred of Jews is inescapable. No reform of the religion is radical enough to avoid such sentiments, and even conversion to Christianity cannot relieve the Jew of this disability. For Hess Jews will always be strangers among the nations – nothing can alter this state of affairs. The only solution is for the Jewish people to come to terms with their identity.

According to Hess, the restoration of Jewish nationalism will not deprive the world of the benefits promoted by Jewish reformers who wish to dissociate themselves from the particularistic aspects of the faith. On the contrary the values of universalism would be championed by various aspects of Judaism's national character. Such a conception, Hess believed, is grounded in the Jewish messianic vision of God's Kingdom on earth. From the beginning of their history, the Jews have been bearers of the faith in a future messianic epoch. What is now required is for Jewry to regenerate the Jewish nation and to keep alive the hope for the political rebirth of the Jewish people. Although not all Jews would be able to emigrate to Palestine, the existence of a Jewish State will act as a spiritual centre for the Jewish people and for all humanity.

The Russian pogroms of 1881 had a profound impact on another early secular Zionist, Leon Pinsker. Born in Tomaszów in Russian Poland in 1821, Pinsker attended a Russian high school, studied law in Odessa, and later received a medical degree from the University of Moscow. Upon returning to Odessa, he was appointed to the staff of the local city hospital. After 1860 Pinsker contributed to Jewish weeklies in the Russian language and was an active member of the Society for the Spread of Culture among the Jews of Russia. However, when Jews were massacred in the pogroms of 1881, he left the society, convinced that a more radical remedy was required to solve the plight of Russian Jewry.

In 1882 Pinsker published *Autoemancipation*, a tract containing similar themes to those found in Hess's writings. Here he asserted that the Jewish problem is as unresolved in modern times as it was in past history. In essence, the dilemma concerns the unassimilable character of Jewry in countries where they are in the minority. In such situations there is no basis for mutual respect between Jews and non-Jews. 'The Jewish people,' he wrote, 'has no fatherland of its own, though many motherlands; it has no rallying point, no centre of gravity, no government of its own, no accredited representatives. It is everywhere a guest, and nowhere at home' (Pinsker, 1932, 6).

Among the nations of the world the Jews are like a people long since dead: the dead walking among the living. Such an eerie, ghostly existence is unique. The fear of the Jewish ghost has been a typical reaction throughout the centuries and has paved the way for current Jew-hatred: 'As a psychic aberration it hereditary; as a disease transmitted for two thousand years, it is incurable' (Pinsker, 1932, 8). Such animosity has generated various charges against the Jewish people – throughout history they have been accused of crucifying Jesus, drinking the blood of Christians, poisoning wells, exacting usury and exploiting peasants. Hence Judaism and anti-Semitism have been inseparable companions through the centuries, and any struggle against this aberration is fruitless.

Unlike other peoples, Pinsker argued, the Jew is a stranger. Having no home, he can never be anything other than an alien. He is not simply a guest in a foreign land, he is rather a beggar and a refugee. The Jews are aliens who can have no representatives because they have no fatherland. It is an error to believe that the legal emancipation of Jewry will result in social emancipation. This is impossible. In summary, he asserted, 'For the living, the Jew is a dead man; for the natives, an alien and a vagrant; for property holders, a beggar; for the poor, an exploiter and millionaire; for patriots, a man without a country; for all classes, a hated rival' (Hertzberg, 1969, 188).

Because of this situation, the Jewish people have no choice but to reconstitute themselves as a separate nation.

The Jewish struggle to attain this goal has, he continues, an inherent justification that belongs to the quest of every oppressed people. Although this quest may be opposed by various quarters, the struggle must continue: the Jewish people have no other way out of their predicament. Jewry needs its own land, but Pinsker pointed out that it would be a mistake for Jews to attach themselves only to Palestine. What is required is simply a secure land for the Jewish nation:

> We need nothing but a large piece of land for our poor brothers; a piece of land which shall remain our property, from which no foreign master can expel us ... Perhaps the Holy Land will again become ours. If so, all the better, but first of all, we must determine ... what country is accessible to us, and at the same time adapted to offer the Jews of all lands who must leave their homes a secure and unquestioned refuge which is capable of being made productive. (Hertzberg, 1969, 194)

More than any other figure, Theodor Herzl has become identified with modern secular Zionism. Born in 1860 in Budapest, he was the only son of a rich merchant. After studying at a technical school and high school in Budapest, he went with his family to Vienna where he studied in the law faculty of the university. In 1884 he obtained a doctorate and worked for a year as a civil servant. Subsequently he wrote plays and joined the staff of the *Neue Freie Presse*. As its Paris correspondent, he witnessed the Dreyfus Affair and became convinced that the Jewish problem could only be solved by the creation of a homeland for Jewry.

After meeting with Baron Maurice de Hirsch to discuss this project, he composed a proposal outlining his views in order to interest the Rothschilds – this became the basis of *The Jewish State* which appeared in February 1896. Herzl's analysis of modern Jewish existence paralleled many of the ideas found in the writings of Hess and Pinsker. Yet what was novel about Herzl's espousal of Zionism was his success in arousing interest and debate about the creation of a Jewish State in the highest diplomatic and political circles.

In the preface to *The Jewish State* Herzl contended that his advocacy of a Jewish homeland is not simply a utopian scheme; on the contrary, this plan is a realistic proposal arising out of the appalling conditions facing Jews in the modern world. According to Herzl, the Jewish question can only be solved if the Jews reconstitute themselves as one people:

> We have sincerely tried everywhere to merge with the national communities in which we live, seeking only to preserve the faith of our fathers. It is not permitted us. In vain are we loyal patriots, sometimes superloyal; in vain do we make the same sacrifices of life and property as our fellow citizens; in vain do we strive to enhance the fame of our native lands in the arts and sciences, or her wealth by trade and commerce. In our native lands where we have lived for centuries we are still decried as aliens ... The majority decide who the 'alien' is; this, and all else in the relations between peoples, is a matter of power. (Hertzberg, 1969, 209)

Old prejudices against the Jewish people are engrained in Western society – assimilation will not cure the ills that beset Jewry. There is only one remedy for the malady of anti-Semitism: the creation of a Jewish commonwealth. In *The Jewish State* Herzl outlined the nature of such a political entity. The plan, he argued, should be carried out by two agencies – the Society of Jews and the Jewish Company. The scientific programme and political policies which the Society of Jews will establish should be carried out by the Jewish Company. This body will be the liquidating agent for the business interests of departing Jews, and will organize trade and commerce in the new country.

Those Jews who agree with this conception of a Jewish state should rally around the Society of Jews and encourage its endeavours. In this way they give it authority in the eyes of governments, and in time ensure that the State is recognized through international law. If other nations were willing to grant Jews sovereignty over a neutral land, then the Society will be able to enter into negotiations for

its possession. Where should this new state be located?
Herzl proposes two alternatives: Palestine or Argentina.
There are advantages for both options, and Herzl asserts
that the Society should take whatever it is given and
whatever Jewish opinion favours.

Here then is a secular reinterpretation of divine deliverance. For writers such as Hess, Pinsker and Herzl, the
redemption of the nation does not depend on the coming
of the Messiah. Rather, in their view Jewry should free
itself from such religious conceptions and work together
to create a homeland where the Jewish people will be
liberated from oppression and persecution. Only by
reconstituting itself as a separate people in its own land
can the Jewish community overcome anti-Semitism.
Although divorced from traditional notions of messianic
deliverance, such a conviction was nonetheless utopian in
character. For secular Zionists, the redemption of the
Jewish people will not take place through a miraculous
intervention, but by means of the establishment of a place
of refuge for the oppressed.

Liberals and Zionists

Paralleling the Orthodox critique of Zionism, liberal Jews
also attacked the Zionists for their utopianism. In their
view, it would be impossible to bring about the emigration
of millions of Jews to Palestine. In addition, in Western
countries nationalism was being supplanted by a vision of a
global community. It was thus reactionary to advocate the
establishment of a Jewish homeland. On the other hand, in
Eastern Europe there was still a vibrant Jewish consciousness. Yet Zionism was unable to solve the problems facing
Jewry: multitudes of Jews in Eastern Europe were enduring
hardship, and only a small minority of these individuals
would be able to settle in *Eretz Israel* (the Land of Israel).
Thus these liberal propagandists stressed that assimilation
alone could serve as a remedy for the Jewish problem.

In response, Zionists argued that assimilation was un-
desirable and inevitably impossible. Such a stance was

influenced by racial theories published before the First World War. According to these studies, distinctive qualities were inherited regardless of social, cultural or economic factors. In the view of the Zionists, the Jewish people constitute an identifiable ethnic group whose identity can not be manipulated through social integration. Anti-Semitism, they maintained, could not be eradicated; it was an inevitable response to the Jewish populace no matter what efforts were made to assimilate Jews into foreign cultures. Moreover, since Jews were predominantly involved in trade and the professions – rather than agriculture and industry – they were bound to be the first targets during times of crisis. Pointing to Jewish history, the Zionists stressed that in the past there were rich and powerful Jews, but without warning they lost their positions in society and were reduced to poverty. There was therefore no security for Jewry living in societies where they were in the minority. Zionism provided the only solution.

Liberals regarded this interpretation of Jewish history as a distortion of the past; previously Jewish emancipation depended on the good will of rulers, but in the modern world it would result from global, socio-economic factors. The Zionists disagreed. The lessons of Jewish history, they argued, must guide current Jewish thought and action. Hostility to Jews is an inherent aspect of contemporary society, and those who champion liberal ideologies such as socialism would be disappointed. In the words of Max Nordeau, the Zionist literary figure and leader:

> Socialism will bring the same disappointments as did the Reformation, the Enlightenment, the movement for political freedom. If we should live to see Socialist theory become practice, you'll be surprised to meet again in the new order that old acquaintance, anti-Semitism. (Laqueur, 1972, 388)

According to Nordeau, the Jew is rootless, and in his address to the First Zionist Congress in 1897, he discussed the social exclusion of Jews in Western countries. Although Jewry was emancipated and enfranchised, he stated they were unable to join gentile clubs and organizations. Everywhere Jews encountered the sign: 'No Jews admitted'. Despite the fact that Jews had been assimilated into foreign cultures, they were not fully accepted. Having dissociated themselves from fellow-Jews, they were rejected by their Christian neighbours. In spite of fleeing from the ghetto, they were not at home in their adopted countries: these new Marranos were strangers, alienated from themselves and their tradition.

Such a depiction of the Jew as a wanderer between two worlds with no home became a dominant theme among Zionist writers. In Germany Moritz Goldstein published an article in 1913 which evoked a storm of controversy. In his view, the Jews held sway over German culture, yet were rejected. Almost all directors of Berlin theatres were Jews; German music was dominated by Jewish artists; literary study was in the hands of Jewish scholars – nevertheless, Jews were viewed as outsiders. What Jews lacked was a native homeland which would provide the soil from which their true greatness could flower. Not surprisingly, Goldstein's opinions were criticized by the liberal establishment.

At this time other voices were also raised against Zionism from throughout the Western world. After Herzl issued his summons to the First Zionist Congress, the executive of the German rabbis issued a declaration stating that the quest to create a Jewish State contradicted messianic longings in the Bible. The Jewish faith, they maintained, obligated the community to serve the countries in which they lived. In France, Joseph Reinarch stated that Zionism was a trap set by anti-Semites for the naive. According to English liberals, Judaism is simply a religion; for this reason British Jews could identify with the society in which they lived. Thus the leader of liberal Judaism in Britain, Claude Montefiore, wrote: 'Liberal Jews do not wish or pray for the restoration of Jews in Palestine' (Laqueur, 1972, 394). Similarly, in the United States liberals denounced Zionists for misreading the modern situation. Thus speaking at the close of the First Zionist Congress, Isaac Mayer Wise, the spokesman for

American Reform Judaism, stated: 'We denounce the whole question of a Jewish state as foreign to the spirit of the modern Jew of this land, who looks upon America as his Palestine and whose interests are centred here' (Laqueur, 1972, 394).

Some of these liberals were anxious to refute the principles of Zionism. For example, Felix Goldman, a German anti-Zionist rabbi, argued that Jewish nationalism is a product of the general chauvinistic movement which had poisoned contemporary history, but would eventually be swept away by universalism. Again, the German Jewish philosopher Hermann Cohen maintained in a debate with the philosopher Martin Buber that Zionism rejected the messianic idea and without this concept there could be no Judaism. In his view, the Zionists were confused about the national issue: Jews were members of the German nation, even if they had different ethnic origins. Other critics went further: Ludwig Geiger, the son of one of the founders of Reform Judaism, asserted that Zionists should be deprived of their civil rights.

Despite such criticisms, Zionism gained many new adherents, and even within the ranks of American Reform Judaism, attempts were made to advance the creation of a Jewish homeland. Nonetheless, resistance to Zionist ideology continued, and in 1942 a number of American anti-Zionists formulated a programme of action. This group claimed that the political policy of the Zionists was at odds with the universalistic interpretation of Jewish history. In their view, Zionism is a secularist movement which undermines the religious nature of Judaism and is out of touch with the universalistic spirit of the faith. Moreover, Zionism threatens Jewry since it calls into question the loyalty of Jews to the countries in which they dwell. In the next year the American Council of Judaism was established to promote such ideas. Its statement of principles declared:

> We oppose the effort to establish a national Jewish State in Palestine or anywhere else as a philosophy of defeatism . . . We dissent from all these related doctrines that stress the racialism, the national and the theoretical homelessness of the

Jews. We oppose such doctrines as inimical to the welfare of Jews in Palestine, in America, or wherever Jews may dwell. (Laqueur, 1972, 404)

Opposition to Zionism did not cease with the founding of the Jewish State. On the contrary, within the ranks of liberal Judaism, a number of writers continued this critique of Zionist ideology. In the 1950s the British Reform rabbi Ignaz Maybaum argued that it is a mistake to believe that Israel is the safest part of the Jewish world. Along similar lines the American Jewish scholar Jacob Petuchowski, writing in the 1960s, stressed that Israel is not the spiritual centre of world Jewry – rather it is one centre among many. For Petuchowski, Judaism is wider than Israel, and an authentic Jewish life is possible elsewhere. Moreover, he stated that the Jewish tradition has continually been influenced by external influences. Hence assimilation is an inherent aspect of the evolving character of the Jewish faith. More recently, however, liberal Judaism worldwide has embraced Israel as a Jewish homeland and spiritual centre. The Nazi Holocaust and the embattled situation of Israel has profoundly altered Jewish consciousness, and the liberal critique of Zionism has now been superseded by a sympathetic appreciation of Jewish aspirations in the Holy Land.

10

Beyond Messianism

Despite the significance of the messianic idea for Jewish life in the past, modern Jews have found it increasingly difficult to believe in a miraculous divine intervention which will change the course of human history. Further, doctrines connected with the coming of the Messiah – including the belief in the resurrection of the dead, the miraculous ingathering of the exiles, final judgment, and reward and punishment in a Hereafter – have seemed totally implausible. With the exception of strictly Orthodox Jews and the Hasidim, most Jews have ceased to adhere to these traditional convictions. Thus it is now necessary to reformulate a new Jewish theology relevant for the modern age. Since biblical times there has been a conscious awareness of the contrast between God as-he-is-in-himself and human perceptions of the Divine. On the basis of this recognition, Jews should free themselves from the absolutes of the past, acknowledging the inevitable subjectivity of religious belief. In this light, Jewish views about the Messiah should be seen as growing out of the life of the people. In the modern world, these ancient doctrines can be superseded by a new vision of Jewish life which is human-centred in orientation. Rather than await the coming of a divinely appointed deliverer who will bring about peace and harmony on earth, Jews should themselves strive to create a better world for all peoples.

The Disintegration of the Messianic Hope

As we have seen, the Hebrew Bible foretells a future redemption of the Jewish people which will be accomplished by an anointed agent of the Lord. For the prophets, such a figure will be a descendant of David who will restore the nation to its former glory. In explaining God's purposes the prophets linked the punishment of the nation with the promise of a future redemption – continually they reassured the people that they would attain future glory. The Apocrypha and Pseudepigrapha amplify these scriptural themes, bearing witness to the longing of the Jewish people for deliverance and redemption. Once the Jews were exiled from the ancient homeland, they were bereft of a country of their own. In their despair they longed for a divinely appointed deliverer who would re-unite them in Zion. In early rabbinic literature the messianic ideas found in Scripture and the Apocrypha and Pseudepigrapha were further developed into a chain of eschatological events including the birth pangs of the Messiah, the emergence of Messiah ben Joseph, the coming of the King-Messiah, the messianic age, final judgment, and the World to Come. Such speculation was accompanied by the arrival of various messianic figures who were perceived by their followers as the long-awaited Messiah. In the first century Jesus' ministry was seen by his disciples as inaugurating the Kingdom of God; a century later the warrior Simeon bar Kochba was viewed by such sages as Rabbi Akiva as the deliverer of the nation. When bar Kochba's revolt against Rome was crushed, Jews put forward the year of messianic redemption to the fifth century. When Moses of Crete failed to bring about an ingathering of the exiles in the middle of this century, Jews continued to speculate about the coming of the Messiah, and during the Middle Ages a series of pseudo-Messiahs proclaimed that the time of deliverance had arrived. Despite the failure of the Messiah to appear, the Jewish community held fast to the belief that messianic deliverance was imminent, and rabbinic scholars in the early modern period continued to speculate about the year of his coming; in addition, a number of false Messiahs appeared during these years. Pre-eminent among these figures was Shabbetai Tzevi whose arrival was extolled throughout the Jewish world. His conversion to

Islam, however, led to widespread despair despite the continuing belief in his Messiahship by various Shabbatean groups.

Not surprisingly the failure of the Messiah to appear through thousands of years of history coupled with the repeated appearance of false Messiahs through the centuries led to widespread disillusionment with the Jewish eschatological hope. As a consequence, the Jewish preoccupation with messianic calculation diminished, and the longing for the Messiah who will lead the Jewish people to the Holy Land and bring about the end of history appeared to many Jews as a misguided aspiration. Instead, eighteenth- and early nineteenth-century Jewry hailed the breaking down of the ghetto walls and the elimination of social barriers between Jews and Christians. In this milieu the belief in the Kingdom of God inaugurated by the Messiah-King receded in importance; in its place the clarion call for liberty, equality, and fraternity signified the dawning of a golden age for the Jewish people.

Within Reform Judaism in particular, the doctrine of messianic redemption was radically modified in the light of these developments. In the nineteenth century Reform Jews tended to interpret the new liberation in the Western world as the first step towards the realization of the messianic dream. For these reformers messianic redemption was understood in this-worldly terms. No longer, according to this view, is it necessary for Jews to pray for a restoration in *Eretz Israel*; rather Jews should view their own countries as Zion and their political leaders as bringing about the messianic age. Such a conviction was enshrined in the Pittsburgh Platform of the Reform movement which was formulated in 1885. As a central principle of the Platform, the belief in a personal Messiah was replaced by the concept of a messianic age which would come about through social causes:

> We recognize in the modern era of universal culture of heart and intellect the approach of the realization of Israel's great messianic hope for the establishment of the kingdom of truth, justice and peace among all men. We consider ourselves

no longer a nation but a religious community, and therefore expect neither a return to Palestine, nor a sacrificial worship under the administration of the sons of Aaron, nor a restoration of any of the laws concerning the Jewish state. (in Plaut, 1965, 34)

These sentiments were shared by secular Zionists who similarly rejected the traditional belief in the coming of the Messiah and the ingathering of the exiles. As we have seen, the early Zionists were determined to create a Jewish homeland even though the Messiah had not yet arrived. Rejecting the religious categories of the Jewish past, such figures as Moses Hess, Leon Pinsker and Theodor Herzl pressed for a political solution to the problem of anti-Semitism. In their view, there is no point in waiting for a supernatural intervention to remedy Jewish existence; rather, Jews must create their own salvation. As Pinsker explained:

Nowadays, when in a small part of the earth our brethren have caught their breath and can feel more deeply for the sufferings of their brothers; nowadays, when a number of other dependent and oppressed nationalities have been allowed to regain their independence, we, too, must not sit even one moment longer with folded hands; we must not admit that we are doomed to play on in the future the hopeless role of the 'wandering Jew' ... it is our bounden duty to devote all our remaining moral force to re-establishing ourselves as a living nation, so that we may finally assume a more fitting and dignified role. (in Hertzberg, 1969, 191)

Such attitudes are representative of a major transformation in Jewish thought. In the past Jews longed for the advent of a personal Messiah who would bring about the messianic age, deliver the Jewish people to their homeland, and inaugurate the fulfilment of human history. Although this doctrine continues to be upheld by a number of devout Orthodox Jews, it has been largely eclipsed by a more secular outlook. Most contemporary Jews prefer to interpret the messianic hope in naturalistic terms, abandoning the belief in the coming of the Messiah, the restoration of the sacrificial system, and the idea of direct divine intervention.

Similarly, most Jews today have set aside other supernatural features of Jewish eschatology which are linked with the messianic hope. The doctrine of the resurrection of the dead has in modern times been generally replaced by the belief in the immortality of the soul. As we have seen, the belief in resurrection was an eschatological belief bound up with the rebirth of the nation in the Days of the Messiah, but as this messianic concept faded into the background so also did this doctrine. For most Jews physical resurrection is simply inconceivable in the light of a scientific understanding of the nature of the world. The late Chief Rabbi, J. H. Hertz, for example, argued that what really matters is the doctrine of the immortality of the soul. Thus he wrote:

> Many and various are the folk beliefs and poetical fancies in the rabbinical writings concerning Heaven, *Gan Eden*, and Hell, *Gehinnom*. Our most authoritative religious guides, however, proclaim that no eye hath seen, nor can mortal fathom, what awaiteth us in the Hereafter; but that even the tarnished soul will not forever be denied spiritual bliss. (in Jacobs, 1988, 415)

In the Reform community a similar attitude prevails. According to the Pittsburgh Platform, Reform Jews

> reassert the doctrine of Judaism that the soul is immortal, grounding this belief on the Divine nature of the human spirit, which forever finds bliss in righteousness and misery in wickedness. We reject as ideas not rooted in Judaism the belief in bodily resurrection and in *Gehenna* and *Eden* (Hell and Paradise) as abodes for eternal punishment or reward. (in Plaut, 1965, 34)

The point to note about the conception of the immortal soul in both Orthodox and Reform Judaism is that it is dissociated from traditional notions of messianic redemption and divine judgment.

The belief in eternal punishment has also been discarded by a large number of Jews, partly because of the interest in penal reform during the past century. Punishment as retaliation in a vindictive sense has been largely rejected. Further, the rabbinic view of Hell is seen by many as morally repugnant. Jewish theologians have stressed that it is a delusion to believe that a God of love could have created a place of eternal punishment. In his commentary on the prayer book, Hertz categorically declared: 'Judaism rejects the doctrine of eternal damnation' (Jacobs, 1988, 415). And in *Jewish Theology* the Reform rabbi, Kaufmann Kohler argued that the question whether the tortures of Hell are reconcilable with divine mercy 'is for us superfluous and superseded. Our modern conceptions of time and space admit neither a place nor a world-period for the reward and punishment of souls, nor the intolerable conception of eternal joy without useful action and eternal agony without any moral purpose' (Kohler, 1968, 309).

Traditional rabbinic eschatology with the Messiah at its centre has thus lost its force for a large number of Jews in the modern period, and in consequence there has been a gradual this-worldly emphasis in Jewish thought. Significantly this has been accompanied by a powerful attachment to the State of Israel. For many Jews the founding of the Jewish State is the central focus of their religious and cultural identity. Jews throughout the world have deep admiration for the astonishing achievements of Israelis in reclaiming the desert and building a viable society, and great respect for the heroism of Israel's soldiers and statesmen. As a result it is not uncommon for Jews to equate Jewishness with Zionism, and to see Judaism as fundamentally nationalistic in character – this is a far cry from the rabbinic view of history which placed the advent of the Messiah at the centre of Jewish life and thought.

A New Theology of Judaism

The collapse of belief in the central aspects of Jewish eschatology has brought about a fundamental change in the life of many Jews: no longer is it possible to subscribe to the religious convictions that supported the community through crisis and tragedy over the centuries. In the light of this transformation, there is thus a pressing need for a reconstructed theology of Judaism for the modern age. What is now required is a religious framework rooted in the tradition which takes account of the contemporary understanding of Divine Reality. In recent years a growing number of thinkers have called for a Copernican revolution in our understanding of the nature of religious belief. Following the distinction between the World-as-Perceived and the World as-it-is-in-itself, these writers argue that Divine Reality as-it-is-in-itself should be distinguished from Divine Reality as conceived in human thought. As John Hick – one of the leading proponents of this view – explains, one should now perceive the great world religions as varying human responses to the one divine reality, embodying different perceptions which have been formed in different historical and cultural circumstances (Hick, 1973, 131).

As far as Judaism is concerned, there has been since biblical times a conscious awareness of the contrast between God as-he-is-in-himself and human perceptions of the Divine. Frequently Scripture cautions against describing God in human terms. As the book of Deuteronomy declares: 'Therefore take good heed to yourselves. Since you saw no form on the day that the Lord spoke to you at Horeb out of the midst of the fire' (Deuteronomy 4:5). Again Exodus 33:20 states:

> 'But', he said, 'You cannot see my face; for man shall not see me, and live.' And the Lord said, 'Behold there is a place by me where you shall stand upon the rock; and while my glory passes by I will put you in a cleft of the rock, and I will cover you with my hand until I have passed by; then I will take away my hand, and you shall see my back; but my face shall not be seen.'

In rabbinic sources there are similar passages which emphasize that human beings should not attempt to describe God. The Palestinian teacher Abin, for example, said: 'When Jacob of the village of Neboria was in Tyre, he interpreted the verse, "For thee, silence is praise, O God" to mean that silence is the ultimate praise of God. It can be compared to a jewel without price: however high you appraise it, you will undervalue it.' In another passage from the Talmud a story is told of the prayer reader who was criticized by the scholar Hanina. This person praised God by listing as many of the divine attributes as he could. When he finished, Hanina asked if he had exhausted the praises of God. Hanina then stated that even the three attributes 'The Great', 'The Valiant' and 'The Tremendous' could not legitimately be used to describe God were it not for the fact that Moses employed them and they later became part of the Jewish liturgy. The text concludes with a parable: if a king who has millions of gold pieces is praised for having millions of silver pieces, such praise actually disparages his wealth rather than glorifies it.

The subsequent development of this view was continued in both the Jewish philosophical and mystical traditions. In his treatise, *Duties of the Heart*, for example, the eleventh-century philosopher, Bahya Ibn Pakudah maintained that the Deity is neither substance nor accident – thus we cannot know God as he is in himself. Rather, it is only through his creatures that we can gain an apprehension of the Divine. According to Bahya, God created the universe *ex nihilo*. From this observation, Bahya went on to discuss God's nature. In his view, the unity of God is not undermined by the ascription to him of divine attributes. In this context Bahya distinguished between essential attributes which are the permanent attributes of God – existence, unity and eternity – and those attributes which are ascribed to God because of his action in the world. For Bahya, the essential attributes should be conceived as negative in character; they deny their opposites. The outcome of this discussion is that only two kinds of attributes are applicable to God: negative attributes and those which we can infer from God's activity as manifest in history.

In the *Guide for the Perplexed*, the twelfth-century Jewish

philosopher Moses Maimonides also discussed the concept of negative attributes. The first part of the *Guide*
begins with a discussion of the anthropomorphic terms in
the Hebrew Scriptures. A literal reading of these passages
suggests that God is corporeal in nature, but according to
Maimonides, this is an error. Such descriptions must be
understood figuratively. In this connection, he argued
that no positive attributes can be predicated of God since
the Divine is an absolute unity. Hence when God is
depicted positively in the Bible, such ascriptions must
refer to his activity. The only true attributes, Maimonides
continued, are negative ones: they lead to a knowledge of
God because in negation no plurality is involved. Each
negative attribute excludes from God's essence some
imperfection. Therefore, when one says that God is incor-
poreal, this means he has no body. Such negation, Maimonides believed, brings one nearer to the knowledge of
the Godhead.

Following Maimonides, the fifteenth-century philosopher Joseph Albo in his *Ikkarim* maintained that those
attributes which refer to God's nature can only be
employed negatively. On the other hand, attributes which
refer to God's acts, can be used positively as long as they
do not imply change in God:

> But even the attributes in this class, those taken from God's
> acts, must be taken in the sense involving perfection, not in
> the sense involving defect. Thus, although these attributes
> cause emotion in us and make us change from one of the
> contraries to the other, they do not necessitate any change or
> emotions in God, for his ways are not our ways, nor are his
> thoughts our thoughts. (in Jacobs, 1973, 41–2)

Like these Jewish philosophers, Jewish mystics advocated a
theology of negation in discussing God's nature. For these
writers the Divine is revealed through the powers which
emanate from him. Yet God as he is in himself is the *Ayn
Sof* (Infinite). As the twelfth-century kabbalist Azriel of
Gerona remarked in his *Maarekhet Ha-Elohut*:

> Know that the *Ayn Sof* cannot be thought of, much less

spoken of, even though there is a hint of it in all things, for there is nothing else apart from it. Consequently, it can be contained neither by letter nor name nor writing nor anything. (in Jacobs, 1973, 43)

In a similar vein the *Zohar* states that the *Ayn Sof* is incomprehensible; it is only through the divine emanations (*sefirot*) that God is manifest in the world. Yet Jewish mystics insisted that the Divine is a unity. Thus a prayer in the *Zohar* ascribed to Elijah emphasizes the unity of the *Ayn Sof* and the *sefirot*:

Elijah began to praise God saying: Lord of the universe! You are one but are not numbered. You are higher than the highest. You are above all mysteries. No thought can grasp you at all. It is you who produced the ten perfections which we call the ten *sefirot*. With them you guide the secret worlds which have not been revealed and the worlds which have been revealed, and in them you conceal yourself from human beings. But it is you who binds them together and unites them. Since you are in them, whoever separates any one of these ten from the others it is as if he had made a division in you. (in Seltzer, 1980, 433)

Here then is a new theological framework deeply embedded in the Jewish tradition which can provide the basis for a new conception of Jewish theology in contemporary society. Acknowledging the limitations of human understanding, such a way of unknowing reveals that there is simply no way to discover the true nature of Divine Reality as-it-is-in-itself. In the end the doctrines of the Jewish faith – including the concept of the Messiah, the ingathering of the exiles, the resurrection of the dead, final judgment, and divine reward and punishment – must be regarded as human images formed from within particular social and cultural contexts. Hence, the absolute claims about God and his activity as found in biblical and rabbinic sources should be understood as human attempts to penetrate the divine mysteries – they all stem from the religious experience of the Jewish nation over centuries of history.

The implications of this shift from the absolutism of the past is of the greatest importance. Judaism, like all other religions, has advanced absolute, universal claims about the nature and activity of God in which the Messiah plays a pivotal role in the unfolding of divine providence. Yet given the inevitable separation between our finite understanding and Ultimate Reality, there is no reason to think that such beliefs are immutable. Divine Reality as-it-is-in-itself transcends human comprehension. It must be admitted, therefore, that Jewish religious convictions are no different in principle from those in other faiths: all are lenses through which the Divine is conceptualized. The collapse of belief in what were previously the central tenets of Jewish eschatology should thus not be seen as a threat to the continuing existence of Judaism, but rather simply as a paradigm shift in modern Jewish consciousness. If the Jewish faith is ultimately a human construct growing out of the experience of the nation over four millennia, it must be susceptible to continuing reinterpretation and change.

Rethinking Jewish Belief

Although Judaism does not contain a formal creed, Maimonides' formulation of the thirteen principles of the Jewish faith has become authoritative for Jewry: as a result these principles are included in most traditional prayer-books in prose form as the *Ani Maamin* prayer. The first of these beliefs deal with the nature of God and his relation to the world and they are followed by doctrines dealing with the advent of the Messiah and the fulfilment of God's eschatological plan:

1. I believe with perfect faith that the creator, blessed be his name, is the author and guide of everything that has been created, and that he alone has made, does make, and will make all things.
2. I believe with perfect faith that the creator, blessed be his name, is a unity, and that there is no unity in any manner like unto his, and that he alone is our God, who was, is, and will be.
3. I believe with perfect faith that the creator, blessed be his name, is not a body, and that he is free from all the

accidents of matter, and that he has not any form whatsoever.

4. I believe with perfect faith that the creator, blessed be his name, is the first and the last.

5. I believe with perfect faith that to the creator, blessed be his name, and to him alone it is right to pray, and that it is not right to pray to any being besides him.

6. I believe with perfect faith that all words of the prophets are true.

7. I believe with perfect faith that the prophecy of Moses our teacher, peace be unto him, was true, and that he was the chief of the prophets, both of those who preceded and of those that followed him.

8. I believe with perfect faith the whole law, now in our possession, is the same that was given to Moses our teacher, peace be unto him.

9. I believe with perfect faith that this law will not be changed, and that there will never be any other law from the creator, blessed be his name.

10. I believe with perfect faith that the creator, blessed be his name, knows every deed of the children of men, and all their thoughts, as it is said, it is he that fashioneth the hearts of them all, that giveth heed to all their deeds (Psalm 33:15).

11. I believe with perfect faith that the creator, blessed be his name, rewards those that keep his commandments, and punishes those that transgress them.

12. I believe with perfect faith in the coming of the Messiah, and though he tarry, I will wait daily for his coming.

13. I believe with perfect faith that there will be a resurrection of the dead at the time when it shall please the creator, blessed be his name, and exalted be the remembrance of him for ever and ever.

In the past traditional Jews regarded such principles as absolute and final. For this reason Maimonides maintained that anyone who denies any of the cardinal beliefs is a heretic: 'When a man breaks away from any of these fundamental principles of belief,' he wrote, 'then of him it is said, "he has gone out of the body of Israel", and he denies the root truth of Judaism.' As a consequence, such individuals will be doomed to eternal punishment: 'Each one ... even if he is an Israelite, has no share in the world to come' (Jacobs, 1988, 15–17).

Such dogmatism, however, is challenged by a new theology of Judaism which acknowledges the inevitable subjectivity of religious belief. On the basis of the distinction between Divine Reality as-it-is-in-itself and Divine Reality as perceived, it is no longer plausible to assert that any religious outlook is categorically true. A theology of Judaism in which religious doctrines are seen as ultimately human in origin demands an attitude of openness and tolerance: absolute claims about Divine Reality should be construed as human conceptions stemming from the experience of the Jewish people through their long history.

On the basis of this understanding, the central tenets of Judaism concerning God's nature and his activity in the universe must be seen as ultimately rooted in the life of the nation. Thus Jewish monotheism – embracing myriad formulations from biblical through medieval to modern times – should be envisaged as grounded in the life of the people. In all cases, pious believers, thinkers and mystics have expressed their understanding of God's nature and activity on the basis of their own spiritual experiences. Yet given that Divine Reality as-it-is-in-itself is ultimately beyond human comprehension, such conceptions should be viewed as only one mode among many different ways of apprehending the Divine. In this light, it makes no sense for Jews to think – as they have in the past – that they possess unique truth about God. On the contrary, universalistic truth-claims should give way to an acknowledgment of the subjectivity of all convictions about Ultimate Reality.

The same conclusion applies to Jewish beliefs about divine revelation. Instead of declaring that God uniquely disclosed his word to the Jewish people in the Hebrew Bible as well as through the teachings of rabbinic sages, Jews should recognize that their Scriptures are simply one record among many others. Both the Written and the Oral Torah have particular significance for Jewry, but this

does not imply that these writings contain a uniquely true
and superior divine revelation. Instead, the Torah as well
as rabbinic literature should be conceived as a record of
the spiritual experiences of the nation and testimony of its
religious quest. For the Jewish people their own sacred
literature has special significance, but it should not be
regarded as possessing truth for all humankind.

Likewise, the doctrine of the chosen people must be
revised. In the past Jews believed that God had selected
them from all nations to be the bearer of his truth.
Although Jews have derived strength from the belief that
God has a special relationship with Israel, such a conviction is based on a misapprehension of Judaism in the
context of the religious experience of the world's faiths.
Given that Divine Reality as-it-is-in-itself transcends
human understanding, the belief that God chose the Jews
as his agent is nothing more than an expression of the
nation's sense of spiritual superiority and impulse to
disseminate its religious message. In fact, however, there
is no way to ascertain if a single group stands in a special
relationship with God.

Again, this new theology of Judaism challenges the
traditional view that God has a providential plan for his
people and for all humanity. The belief that God's guid-
ance is manifest in all things is ultimately grounded in a
human response to the universe: it is not, as Jews have
believed through the centuries, certain knowledge. This is
illustrated by the fact that other faiths have proposed a
similar view of both general and special providence, yet
contend that God's action in the world has taken an
entirely different course. In other cases, non-theistic religions (such as Buddhism) have formulated conceptions
of human destiny divorced from the intervention of God
or the gods. Such differences in orientation highlight the
subjective nature of all belief systems.

The Jewish conception of messianic deliverance must
also be understood in a similar light: the longing for a
personal Messiah should be perceived as a pious hope
based on both personal and communal expectations.

Although this conviction has served as a bedrock of the Jewish religion since biblical times, it is inevitably shaped by human conceptualization. Thus, like all other doctrines in Judaism, it is grounded in the experience of the Jewish nation and has undergone a variety of reformulations in the course of the history of the nation. Yet, because Divine Reality as-it-is-in-itself is beyond human understanding, there is no way of determining whether the belief in the Messiah is valid.

Further, this new understanding of Judaism demands a similar stance concerning the doctrine of the afterlife. Although the belief in the eschatological unfolding of history has been a central feature of the Jewish heritage from rabbinic times to the present, it is simply impossible to ascertain whether these events will in fact occur in the future. In our finite world, limited by space and time, certain knowledge about such issues is unobtainable. Belief in the hereafter in which the righteous of Israel will receive their just reward has sustained the Jewish people through suffering, persecution and tragedy, yet this doctrine can be no more certain than any other elements of the Jewish religious tradition.

The implications of this shift from the absolutism of the past to a new vision of Judaism are radical and far reaching. In the past Jews have advanced absolute, universal truth claims about the nature of the world, but given the separation between our finite understanding of the Divine as-it-is-in-itself, there can be no way of attaining certainty about the veracity of these beliefs. Divine Reality transcends human comprehension; hence it must be admitted that Jewish religious beliefs are in principle no different from those found in other religious traditions – all are lenses through which the Divine is conceptualized. In its various forms – like all the world religions – the Jewish faith is built around its distinctive way of thinking and experiencing Divine Reality. In summary, this reformulation of Jewish theology provides a fundamentally new framework for understanding the nature of Jewish belief: religious dogmas in Judaism should be perceived, not as a systematic presentation of truths about God's nature and his relation to the world, but rather as a projection of socially and culturally conditioned views of the Divine.

Towards Human Empowerment

As we have seen, from biblical times to the modern age the Jewish community anticipated the coming of the Messiah who would redeem the nation from earthly travail and usher in a new era of peace. As we have seen, this doctrine underwent considerable development over time, yet despite the various interpretations of messianic deliverance, its central affirmation remained constant: human history will find its ultimate fulfilment in a future age when cosmic harmony will be restored. Despite the centrality of messianic belief in the history of the nation, the modern period has witnessed the disintegration of this doctrine. Increasingly Jews have found it difficult, if not impossible, to believe in the advent of messianic redemption. With the exception of the strictly Orthodox as well as the Hasidim, most Jews have abandoned the Jewish eschatological picture of divine redemption.

Two major factors have led to this change in attitude. In contemporary society it has become apparent that both biblical and rabbinic conceptions of the universe were based on a pre-scientific and mistaken understanding of nature. As a result of the expansion of scientific knowledge, most modern Jews are unable to accept the scriptural account and subsequent rabbinic view of the origin of the universe as well as God's activity in the world. The climate of thought in the twentieth century is thus one in which scientific explanation has taken over the role of religious interpretation.

Although the sciences have not disproved the claims of Judaism, they have provided a rational explanation of events that were previously seen as the result of divine agency. In this light religious convictions have been perceived as subjective in origin, to be ousted eventually from the central areas of human knowledge. In other words, the sciences have effectively established the autonomy of the natural world. Nature is studied without any reference to God, and the universe is investigated as though the Deity does not exist. In essence, the contemporary period has witnessed scientific advance on the one hand and the retreat of traditional belief on the other.

A second factor which has brought about the eclipse of Jewish theism is the fact of evil. For many Jews today, the existence of human suffering makes the idea of an all-good and all-powerful God utterly implausible: after the events of the Holocaust, the traditional belief that God is a loving father who watches over his chosen people has become impossible to sustain. In modern society, faith in such a Deity has been overshadowed by an overwhelming sense that the universe is devoid of a divine presence. The views of the radical Jewish theologian, Richard Rubenstein, reflect the attitude of a large segment of the Jewish community. In *After Auschwitz*, he wrote:

> When I say that we live in the time of the death of God, I mean that the thread uniting God and man, Heaven and Earth, has been broken. We stand in a cold, silent, unfeeling cosmos, unaided by any powerful power beyond our own resources. After Auschwitz, what else can a Jew say about God? (Rubenstein, 1966, 151–2)

A new consciousness is therefore needed which is in tune with this shift in outlook. As we have seen, a growing number of contemporary thinkers have drawn attention to the inevitable subjectivity of religious belief; in their view, the world faiths should be understood as different human responses to the Divine. In the light of this interpretation, Jewish views of divine deliverance, final judgment, resurrection of the dead, and reward and punishment should be seen as rooted in the life of the nation rather than ultimate truths which have been revealed from on high. Such a transformation of perspective calls for a revolutionary change in Jewish life and thought. In the past the community looked to God for release from their travail. In the biblical period, the prophets reassured the nation that God would not forsake his chosen people; subsequently the nation awaited the arrival of a descendant of King David who would restore Israel to its former glory. In the exile which followed the destruction of the Temple in 70 CE, the Jewish people longed for the coming of a messianic redeemer who would lead them back from exile. Coupled with this belief was the conviction that the righteous would be rewarded in the World to Come. Through centuries of persecution and tragedy the community was consoled by such convictions.

Today, however, such longing for supernatural intervention should be seen as a pious hope nurtured through centuries of persecution and tragedy; rather than wait for the Messiah to come to redeem the world, Jews should now rely on themselves to shape their own destiny. Within the Jewish community, two religious movements – Reconstructionism and Humanistic Judaism – have embraced such a naturalistic interpretation of the faith. According to Mordecai Kaplan, the founder of Reconstructionist Judaism, it no longer makes sense to believe in a supernatural Deity. In his view, God is not a supernatural being, but the power that makes for salvation. 'God,' he wrote, 'is the sum of all the animating, organizing forces and relationships which are forever making a cosmos out of chaos' (Kaplan, 1962, 76). In his view, the idea of God must be understood in terms of its effect:

> We learn more about God when we say that love is divine than when we say God is love. A veritable transformation takes place ... Divinity becomes relevant to authentic experience and therefore takes on a definiteness which is accompanied by an awareness of authenticity. (Kaplan, 1970, 73).

In order for Judaism to survive, Kaplan continued, it must divest itself of traditional views of God, and the spiritual dimension of the faith must be reformulated in humanistic terms. Speaking of salvation, he wrote:

> When religion speaks of salvation it means in essence the experience of the worthwhileness of life. When we analyse

our personal experience of life's worthwhileness we find that
it is invariably based on specific ethical experiences – moral
responsibility, honesty, loyalty, love, service. If carefully pur-
sued, this analysis reveals that the source of our ethical
experience is found in our willingness and ability to achieve
self-fulfilment through reciprocity with others. This reciprocity in turn is an expression of a larger principle that operates
in the cosmos in response to the demands of a cosmic force
that makes for creativity and interdependence in all things.
(Kaplan, 1970, 70)

Similarly, for Humanistic Jews it no longer makes sense to
believe in a God who saves. Rather than subscribe to
traditional notions of divine deliverance through a messianic agent, Humanistic Judaism asserts that Jews must
rely on themselves. For this reason, the movement emphasizes the importance of humanistic values:

We believe in the value of human reason and in the validity of
the world which reason discloses. The natural universe stands
on its own, requiring no supernatural intervention. We
believe in the value of human experience and in the power of
human beings to solve their problems both individually and
collectively. Life should be directed to the satisfaction of
human needs. Every person is entitled to life, dignity and
freedom. We believe in the value of Jewish identity and in the
survival of the Jewish people. Jewish history is a human story.
Judaism, as the civilization of the Jews, is a human creation.
Jewish identity is an ethnic reality. The civilization of the
Jewish people embraces all manifestations of Jewish life,
including Jewish languages, ethical traditions, historic mem-
ories, cultural heritage, and especially the emergence of the
state of Israel in modern times. Judaism also embraces many
belief systems and lifestyles. As the creation of the Jewish
people in all ages, it is always changing. We believe in the
value of a secular humanistic democracy for Israel and for all
the nations of the world. Religion and state must be separate.
The individual right to privacy and moral autonomy must be
guaranteed. Equal rights must be granted to all, regardless of
race, sex, creed or ethnic origin. (in Cohn-Sherbok, 1996, 156)

Here then are two important developments in the Jewish
world which reflect the shift in orientation away from

traditional Jewish understanding of salvation to a this-worldly humanistic viewpoint. Even though only a small segment of Jews belongs to either the Reconstructionist or Humanistic branches of Judaism, many have either consciously or unconsciously accepted the change of attitude that these movements endorse. The Jewish people are thus on the verge of a new awakening as the twentieth century reaches its climax: rather than rely on the miraculous intervention of a messianic redeemer who will inaugurate a time of earthly bliss and bring about the consummation of human history, Jews are coming to accept that the burden of creating a better world rests ultimately with themselves. Out of the ashes of the past then, the vision of a human-centred Judaism has emerged: this is not a fatal tragedy for the nation, but rather a challenge to reflection and action on the threshold of a new millennium.

Conclusion

For over three thousand years Jews have longed for divine redemption. As Scripture records, God promised the patriarchs that their descendants would be secure in their own land; subsequently the prophets foretold of a future redemption which would be ushered in through an anointed agent of the Lord. This kingly figure, they maintained, would be a descendant of King David. In time there arose the view that this figure would rule over both kingdoms. In the eighth century the Northern prophets warned the nation that it would be destroyed because of Israel's iniquity, yet they predicted that the people would endure. This message of destruction and restoration continued in the ministries of later pre-exilic prophets: in their view God would not bring about a new redemption for the survivors. Later in the post-exilic period this message of hope was repeated by other prophets who reassured the nation that it would be restored through the coming of a divinely appointed deliverer who would be given dominion over all the earth. The theme of divine redemption continued throughout the Second Temple period. In the Apocrypha the concept of a future world in which the righteous will be rewarded was developed and elaborated. Dating from a later period, the Pseudepigrapha are filled with messianic longing. In these works the Day of Judgment, the birth pangs of the Messiah, the personality of the Messiah ben David, and the Days of the Messiah are described in detail. Although the messianic predictions in these writings vary considerably, these works vividly illustrate the continuing longing for divine deliverance.

Once the Temple had been destroyed, the Jewish people were driven into exile; in their despair they longed for the coming of the Messiah who would return them to their ancient homeland and rebuild Jerusalem. Drawing on ideas found in the Hebrew Bible as well as the Apocrypha and Pseudepigrapha, the rabbis envisaged the coming of a future redemption when all nations would recognize the God of Israel. Such ideas encouraged speculation about God's eschatological plan. According to various sages, the messianic age will be brought about through righteous actions. Nonetheless, prior to the coming of the Messiah, the world would be subject to tumultuous events referred to as 'the birth pangs of the Messiah'; these will be followed by the arrival of a forerunner of the Messiah, and then a second figure, Messiah ben Joseph, who will engage in battle with Israel's enemies. After his death, a King-Messiah will arrive who will bring about the transformation of human history. Through his intervention all human beings will be judged, and the righteous will be rewarded. This vision of a future hope was animated by the belief that God would redeem his chosen people as he had promised in ancient times.

Such speculation intensified the Jewish longing for the coming of the Messiah who will bring about the restoration of the kingdom. In this milieu, a Jewish sect emerged during the years following Herod's death, which believed that Jesus would usher in the era of messianic deliverance. Attracting adherents from among the most marginalized sectors of Jewish society, Jesus soon aroused hostility and was put to death during the reign of Pontius Pilate. Nonetheless, his disciples believed he had risen from the dead and will return to reign in glory. For his followers Jesus was perceived as the long-awaited Messiah; as God's anointed, he ushered in the Kingdom of God in which the old Torah is superseded. Forgiveness, atonement, and salvation are offered through God's redemptive intervention in human history. This vision of messianic deliverance brought about by Jesus is, however, at odds with traditional Judaism. To the Jewish mind, God's covenant

Conclusion   193

with the Jews is intact: the Messiah has not yet come, and because of the differences of understanding of the role of the Messiah, Judaism and Christianity have gone their separate ways through the centuries.

Although the Jewish community rejected Jesus as the long-awaited Messiah, Jews continued to long for redemption. Hence, in the next century when a revolt took place against Rome, its leader – Simeon bar Kochba – was perceived by many Jews as a messianic deliverer of the nation. When this uprising was crushed and Simeon killed in battle, the advent of the Messiah was put forward until the fifth century. In about 448 a messianic figure named Moses appeared in Crete, declaring he would lead the Jews across the sea to the Holy Land. After his plan failed, Jews continued to engage in messianic speculation and their reflections are recorded in a number of midrashic works of the next few centuries. In the ninth century the scholar Saadiah Gaon calculated the date of final redemption on the basis of biblical sources. During these centuries of heightened messianic awareness, a number of false Messiahs – Abu Isa al-Ispahani, Serene, and Yudghan – appeared, and the traveller Eldad Ha-Dani brought news of the ten lost tribes which further stimulated Jewish longing for a return to Zion.

As time passed, Jewish aspirations for deliverance intensified. As a result, when the Crusades occurred Jews viewed the massacres of the community as the birth pangs of the Messiah. In subsequent years the same longing for redemption and return to Zion was expressed by Jews who continued to suffer at the hands of Christians. In the next two centuries a number of Jewish writers sought to determine the date of messianic redemption on the basis of verses in the Book of Daniel; prominent among these scholars was Solomon ibn Gabirol, Rashi, Judah Halevi, and Abraham bar Hiyya. During this period several pseudo-Messiahs appeared. Previously such figures came from Asia Minor, Babylonia and Persia, but with the shift of Jewry to Mediterranean countries, false Messiahs were found also in Western Europe. The most important pseudo-Messiah of this period was David Alroy who was viewed by his followers as the saviour of Israel. In the following centuries messianic calculators continued to speculate about the coming of the Messiah on the basis of the Hebrew Bible. Frequently they relied on kabbalistic forms of exegesis in their computations. Mystical works of this era such as the *Zohar* also contained reflections about the advent of the messianic age. In the thirteenth century another messianic figure, Abraham Abulafia, appeared on the scene.

During the fourteenth and fifteenth centuries the Jewish community continued to long for the Messiah who would return the Jewish people to their homeland, despite his failure to appear in 1348 and 1403. These centuries witnessed the production of messianic treatises, and such scholars as Simeon ben Zemah Duran and Isaac Abrabanel speculated about the year of his coming. The tradition of messianic calculation was practised in the next century by other scholars; in addition, during this period several false Messiahs such as David Reuveni and Solomon Molko appeared. Undaunted by the failure of these figures to usher in the messianic age, messianic calculators of the seventeenth century persisted in their investigations. Pre-eminent among the writers of this period was Manasseh ben Israel who believed that the hour of deliverance was near. The Cossack Rebellion which began in 1648 and devastated Polish Jewry heightened the belief that the coming of the Messiah was close at hand. In 1665 the arrival of the self-proclaimed messianic king, Shabbetai Tzevi, was announced by his disciple Nathan of Gaza. Throughout the world, Jewry was electrified. Yet when Shabbetai converted to Islam rather than face death, his apostasy evoked widespread despair. Nevertheless, a number of his followers continued to adhere to his claim of messiahship, and a schismatic group of his disciples (the *Doenmeh*) broke away from mainstream Judaism. Later in the eighteenth century the Shabbatean movement was led by Jacob Frank who became the head of the Frankists, an heretical sect which continued to subscribe to a version of the Shabbatean kabbalistic tradition.

With the conversion of Shabbetai Tzevi the Jewish interest in messianic calculation generally diminished. Nonetheless a number of traditional Jews continued to subscribe to the belief in the advent of the messianic era, coupling this conviction with the desire to rebuild *Eretz Israel*. Prominent among such religious Zionists of the nineteenth century was Yehuda hai Alkalai who argued that Jewish settlers should establish Jewish colonies in Palestine in anticipation of the coming of the Messiah. Similarly, Zwi Hirsch Kalischer maintained that the messianic era will not take place immediately; rather the redemption of the Jewish people will occur gradually through the ingathering of the Jewish nation in their ancestral home. Later Abraham Isaac Kook attempted to harmonize messianic aspirations with the actions of modern secular Zionists. Deeply disturbed by this reinterpretation of messianic redemption, Orthodox critics argued that Zionism in any form is a betrayal of the tradition. According to these opponents, it is forbidden to accelerate divine redemption through human efforts. Other Jews, however, adopted an entirely secular approach to Jewish nationalism. Rejecting the belief in messianic deliverance, the early Zionists argued that only by creating their own nation will Jews be able to solve the problem of anti-Semitism. Finally, liberal Jews attacked both secular and messianic Zionism, maintaining that Jews should seek to assimilate into the countries in which they live rather than create a country of their own.

Despite the significance of belief in messianic redemption within traditional Judaism, the modern world has witnessed the gradual erosion of the concept of the Messiah. With the exception of the strictly Orthodox and the Hasidim, Jews today have found it increasingly difficult to accept the traditional scheme of eschatological salvation. Such a shift in perspective is largely due to increased secularism and the impact of science on the Jewish mind. No longer do most Jews subscribe to the fundamental principles of the Jewish faith as outlined by Maimonides and enshrined in the *Yigdal*. In this light, what is now needed is a new theology of Judaism which takes account of this shift in religious perspective. As argued in the last chapter, such a revised Jewish theology would accept the inevitable subjectivity of religious belief. Because all believers are limited by human understanding and perception, there can be no way of ascertaining the true nature of Divine Reality. On such a view, neither Judaism nor any other religion contains an absolute and universally valid conception of the Divine. Rather in each case, the view of Divine Reality is conditioned by such factors as history, language and culture. For these reasons the doctrine of Divine Reality is characteristically different in every case.

Within this new theological framework, the absolute claims about God, the Messiah, divine redemption, the ingathering of the exiles, and the World to Come should be understood as human conceptions stemming from the religious experience of the ancient Israelites as well as later generations of Jewish sages. In the past such beliefs sustained the nation through tragedy and death, yet with the eclipse of belief in Jewish eschatology and the recognition of the inevitable subjectivity of religious doctrine, they should now be replaced by an emphasis on the importance of human action. Such a transformation in orientation can be represented diagramatically. As we have seen, in previous centuries the messianic hope was at the centre of Jewish life:

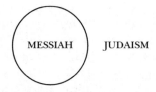

Today, however, such a messianic-centred conception of Judaism should be replaced by a human-centred model of

Jewish existence which acknowledges that the belief system of the Jewish faith is ultimately a human construction; such a notion of Judaism would also highlight the significance of human action in the world as opposed to the messianic hope for the coming of a divinely appointed deliverer who will redeem all humankind:

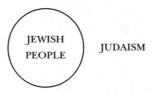

Hence, despite the meaningfulness of the concept of the Messiah for Jewish existence in the past, the messianic idea of divine deliverance as presented in the Hebrew Bible, post-biblical writings and rabbinic sources should be set aside. Instead of looking to a heavenly form of redemption, the Jewish community must now rely on itself for its own survival and the redemption of the world. Such a reorientation of the faith can be summarized by a new Credo for the Post-Messianic Age.

A Post-Messianic Credo

1. I believe that in biblical times the belief in the Messiah sustained the ancient Israelites through the destruction of both the Northern and Southern Kingdoms. With the fall of Jerusalem in 70 CE, the messianic hope served as a utopian ideal which enabled the Jewish people to remain faithful to God. Assured of divine deliverance and ultimate redemption in the World to Come, the Jewish community was able to face persecution, tragedy and death.

2. I believe that, despite the significance of the process of messianic redemption in the life of the Jewish nation, it must be recognized that Jewish eschatological beliefs are human in origin. Paralleling the development of religious doctrines in other faiths, the messianic idea was

elaborated by sages and scholars to provide an explanation for God's dealing with his chosen people.

3.   I believe that the attempt of Jewish scholars in previous
     centuries to determine the date of the advent of the
     Messiah was a pious, though misguided quest.

4.   I believe that the various Jewish messianic figures of the
     past were all pseudo-Messiahs; despite the sincerity of
     their followers, these messianic pretenders suffered
     from a delusion about their messianic role.

5.   I believe that, given the subjective character of messianic
     belief, it makes more sense for Jews today to set aside the
     hope for final deliverance and redemption through a
     divine agent who will usher in a period of peace and
     harmony and bring about the end of history.

6.   I believe that, with the demise of the messianic hope,
     the Jewish people must look to themselves for survival. It
     is only through the actions of the nation on its own
     behalf that a Jewish future can be secured. After the
     destruction of six million Jews in the Holocaust, it has
     become clear that Jewry must remain ever vigilant to
     protect itself from its enemies.

7.   I believe that the State of Israel, as a symbol of Jewish
     vitality in a post-Holocaust world, is of central impor-
     tance for the Jewish community. Now established in its
     ancient homeland, the Jewish people has a means to
     safeguard itself from destruction. Modern Zionism – as a
     conscious rejection of the messianic promise of return
     from exile – has brought to the Jewish people renewed
     hope for the future.

8.   I believe that the humanistic values of the Jewish herit-
     age should serve as guiding principles for regulating
     national affairs within the Jewish State. Israel's political
     policies should not be determined solely on the basis of
     realpolitik; instead ethical ideals rooted in the tradition
     should be at the forefront of the nation's decision-
     making.

9.   I believe that Jews in the diaspora have the responsibility
     to engage in social action; the quest to create a better
     world through human endeavour is at the heart of the
     Jewish faith. Jews today must actively engage in this
     process rather than wait for a miraculous divine inter-
     vention to bring about peace and harmony on earth.

10. I believe that in the struggle to ameliorate society Jews should look beyond their own community. Together with members of other faiths, they should strive to improve the lives of all human beings and the world they live in.

Here then is a new humanistic creed for Post-Messianic Judaism. In place of the messianic vision of an unfolding providential scheme leading to divine reward and punishment in the Hereafter, this Credo envisages Jewish existence as determined by the Jewish people themselves. Although such a human-centred perspective is far removed from the religious ideals of the past, it is consistent with the outlook of most Jews today – as such, it provides a realistic basis for Jewish living in a secular and scientific age.

Bibliography

Ackroyd, P., *Exile and Restoration*, London, 1968

Anderson, B. W., *The Eighth Century Prophets*, London, 1979

Avineri, S., *The Making of Modern Zionism: The Intellectual Origins of the Jewish State*, New York, 1981

Baeck, L., *The Essence of Judaism*, New York, 1948

Baile, D., *Power and Powerlessness in Jewish History*, New York, 1979

Bamberger, B., *The Story of Judaism*, New York, 1964

Baron, S. W., *A Social and Religious History of the Jews*, New York, 1952–76

Ben-Sasson, H. H., *A History of the Jewish People*, Cambridge, 1976

Bright, J., *A History of Israel*, London and Philadelphia, 1972

Buber, M., *Zion: The History of an Idea*, Edinburgh, 1985

Cohn, N., *In Pursuit of the Millennium*, New York, 1970

Cohn-Sherbok, D., *Modern Judaism*, London, 1996

Cohn-Sherbok, D., *Jewish Mysticism: An Anthology*, New York, 1995

Cohn-Sherbok, D., *Jewish and Christian Mysticism*, New York, 1994

Cohn-Sherbok, D., *The Jewish Faith*, London, 1993

Cohn-Sherbok, D., *Israel: The History of an Idea*, London, 1992

Cohn-Sherbok, D., *Issues in Contemporary Judaism*, London, 1991

Cohn-Sherbok, D., *Holocaust Theology*, London, 1989

Davidson, I. (ed.), *Selected Religious Poetry of Solomon ibn Gabirol*, 1923

Davies, W. D., *The Territorial Dimension of Judaism*, Berkeley, 1982

de Lange, N., *Judaism*, Oxford, 1986

Drane, J., *Introducing the New Testament*, Tring, 1986

Encyclopedia Judaica, Jerusalem, 1972

Epstein, I., *Judaism*, London, 1975

Eusebius, *The History of the Church*, Baltimore, 1965

Ginzberg, L. *Legends of the Jews*, Philadelphia, 1968

Grant, M., *The History of Ancient Israel*, New York, 1984

Graetz, H. *History of the Jews*, Philadelphia, 1967

Gressman, H., *Der Messias*, Göttingen, 1929

Gubbay, L., *Quest for the Messiah*, Sussex, 1990

Hertzberg, A. (ed.), *The Zionist Idea: A Historical Analysis and Reader*, New York, 1969

Hick, J., *God and the Universe of Faiths*, New York, 1973

Husik, I., *History of Medieval Jewish Philosophy*, Philadelphia, 1958

Jacobs, L., *Principles of the Jewish Faith*, Northvale, N.J., 1988

Jacobs, L., *Jewish Mystical Testimonies*, New York, 1977

Jacobs, L., A *Jewish Theology*, New York, 1973

Jewish Encyclopaedia, New York, 1901–5

Johnson, P., *A History of the Jews*, London, 1987

Kaplan, M., 'The Meaning of God for the Contemporary Jew' in A. Jospe (ed.), *Tradition and Contemporary Experience*, New York, 1970

Kaplan, M., *The Meaning of God in Modern Jewish Religion*, New York, 1962

Kaplan, M., *Judaism as a Civilization*, New York, 1967

Katz, J., *Exclusiveness and Tolerance*, New York, 1962

Klausner, J., *The Messianic Idea in History*, London, 1956

Kohler, K., *Jewish Theology*, New York, 1968

Kumar, K., *Utopia and Anti-Utopia in Modern Times*, Oxford, 1962

Laqueur, W., *A History of Zionism*, New York, 1972

Lindbloom, J., *Prophecy in Ancient Israel*, Oxford, 1962

Margolis, M. L., and Marx, A., *A History of the Jewish People*, Philadelphia, 1927

Meyer, M., *Response to Modernity: A History of the Reform Movement in Judaism*, Oxford, 1988

Montefiore, C. G. and Loewe, H. (eds.), *A Rabbinic Anthology*, New York, 1964

O'Brien, C. C., *The Siege: The Saga of Israel and Zionism*, London, 1986

Pinsker, L., *Autoemancipation*, London, 1932

Plaut, G. W. (ed.), *The Growth of Reform Judaism*, New York, 1965

Plaut, G. W. (ed.), *The Rise of Reform Judaism*, New York, 1963

Rubenstein, R. L., *After Auschwitz*, Indiana, 1966

Rubenstein, R. L. and Roth, J., *Approaches to Auschwitz*, London, 1987

Sachar, A. L., *A History of the Jews*, New York, 1967

Sacks, J., *One People? Tradition, Modernity and Jewish Unity*, London, 1993

Sarachek, J., *The Messianic Ideal in Medieval Jewish Literature*, New York, 1932

Scholem, G., *Sabbatai Sevi: The Mystical Messiah*, Princeton, 1973

Scholem, G., *The Messianic Idea in Judaism*, New York, 1971

Scholem, G., *Major Trends in Jewish Mysticism*, New York, 1946

Seltzer, R., *Jewish People, Jewish Thought: The Jewish Experience in History*, London, 1980

Silver, A. H., *A History of Messianic Speculation in Israel*, Gloucester, Mass., 1978

Super, A., *Immortality in the Babylonian Talmud* (unpublished PhD. thesis, 1967)

Trepp, L., *A History of the Jewish Experience*, New York, 1973

Vital, D., *The Future of the Jews*, Cambridge, Mass., 1990

Vital, D., *The Origins of Zionism*, Oxford, 1975

Wine, S., *Judaism Beyond God*, Detroit, Michigan, 1985

Glossary

Amidah	central prayer of the Jewish liturgy
Avot	sayings of the Fathers
Ayn Sof	infinite
Baraitha	rabbinic commentary or legal material not included in the *Mishnah*
Devekut	cleaving to God
Doenmeh	Judeo-Muslim sect of the seventeenth century
Gan Eden	Heaven
Gehinnom	Hell
Gematria	exegesis based on the numerical value of Hebrew words
Halakhah	Jewish law
Ha-Meshiah	the Messiah
Hasidei Ashkenaz	German medieval scholars
Haskalah	Jewish enlightenment
Herem	excommunication
Kabbalah	Jewish mysticism
Kelippot	powers of evil
Kinnot	prayers of lamentation
Matzot	unleavened bread
Midrash	rabbinic commentary on Scripture
Mishnah	second-century rabbinic code
Mitnagdim	rabbinic opponents of the Hasidim
Nagid	head of the Jewish community in Islamic countries
Notarikon	exegesis based on the letters of a word as an abbreviation of sentences
Piyyut	liturgical poem

Rebbe	Hasidic spiritual leader
Sefirot	divine emanations
Selihot	penitential prayers
Shavuot	Festival of Weeks
Shekinah	Divine presence
Shema	major prayer of the Jewish liturgy ('Hear, O Israel')
Sukkot	Festival of Tabernacles or Booths
Talmud	Discussion of the Oral Law based on the *Mishnah*
Tannaim	rabbinic scholars of the mishnaic period
Tikkun	cosmic repair
Tzimtzum	Divine contraction
Yeshivah	rabbinical academy
Yigdal	Jewish prayer
Zaddik	Hasidic spiritual leader
Zeruf	exegesis of Scripture based on the combination of letters
Zohar	medieval mystical text

Index